New York Academic Content Standards

Standard 1 Social Studies: History of the United States and New York

Students will: use a variety of intellectual skills to demonstrate their understanding of major ideas, eras, themes, developments, and turning points in the history of the United States and New York.

1.1 The study of New York State and United States history requires an analysis of the development of American culture, its diversity and multicultural context, and the ways people are unified by many values, practices, and traditions.

1.2 Important ideas, social and cultural values, beliefs, and traditions from New York State and United States history illustrate the connections and interactions of people and events across time and from a variety of perspectives.

1.3 Study about the major social, political, economic, cultural, and religious developments in New York State and United States history involves learning about the important roles and contributions of individuals and groups.

1.4 The skills of historical analysis include the ability to: explain the significance of historical evidence; weigh the importance, reliability, and validity of evidence; understand the concept of multiple causation; understand the importance of changing and competing interpretations of different historical developments.

Standard 2 Social Studies: World History

Students will: use a variety of intellectual skills to demonstrate their understanding of major ideas, eras, themes, developments, and turning points in world history and examine the broad sweep of history from a variety of perspectives.

2.1 The study of world history requires an understanding of world cultures and civilizations, including an analysis of important ideas, social and cultural values, beliefs, and traditions. This study also examines the human condition and the connections and interactions of people across time and space and the ways different people view the same event or issue from a variety of perspectives.

2.2 Establishing timeframes, exploring different periodizations, examining themes across time and within cultures, and focusing on important turning points in world history help organize the study of world cultures and civilizations.

2.3 Study of the major social, political, cultural, and religious developments in world history involves learning about the important roles and contributions of individuals and groups.

2.4 The skills of historical analysis include the ability to investigate differing and competing interpretations of the theories of history, hypothesize about why interpretations change over time, explain the importance of historical evidence, and understand the concepts of change and continuity over time.

Standard 3 Social Studies: Geography

Students will: use a variety of intellectual skills to demonstrate their understanding of the geography of the interdependent world in which we live—local, national, and global—including the distribution of people, places, and environments over the Earth's surface.

3.1 Geography can be divided into six essential elements which can be used to analyze important historic, geographic, economic, and environmental questions and issues. These six elements include: the world in spatial terms, places and regions, physical settings (including natural resources), human systems, environment and society, and the use of geography. (Adapted from The National Geography Standards, 1994: Geography for Life)

3.2 Geography requires the development and application of the skills of asking and answering geographic questions; analyzing theories of geography; and acquiring, organizing, and analyzing geographic information. (Adapted from: The National Geography Standards, 1994: Geography for Life)

Standard 4 Social Studies: Economics

Students will: use a variety of intellectual skills to demonstrate their understanding of how the United States and other societies develop economic systems and associated institutions to allocate scarce resources, how major decision-making units function in the U.S. and other national economies, and how an economy solves the scarcity problem through market and nonmarket mechanisms.

4.1 The study of economics requires an understanding of major economic concepts and systems, the principles of economic decision making, and the interdependence of economies and economic systems throughout the world.

4.2 Economics requires the development and application of the skills needed to make informed and well-reasoned economic decisions in daily and national life.

Standard 5 Social Studies: Civics, Citizenship, and Government

Students will: use a variety of intellectual skills to demonstrate their understanding of the necessity for establishing governments; the governmental system of the U.S. and other nations; the U.S. Constitution; the basic civic values of American constitutional democracy; and the roles, rights, and responsibilities of citizenship, including avenues of participation.

5.1 The study of civics, citizenship, and government involves learning about political systems; the purposes of government and civic life; and the differing assumptions held by people across time and place regarding power, authority, governance, and law. (Adapted from The National Standards for Civics and Government, 1994)

5.2 The state and federal governments established by the Constitutions of the United States and the State of New York embody basic civic values (such as justice, honesty, self-discipline, due process, equality, majority rule with respect for minority rights, and respect for self, others, and property), principles, and practices and establish a system of shared and limited government. (Adapted from The National Standards for Civics and Government, 1994)

5.3 Central to civics and citizenship is an understanding of the roles of the citizen within American constitutional democracy and the scope of a citizen's rights and responsibilities.

5.4 The study of civics and citizenship requires the ability to probe ideas and assumptions, ask and answer analytical questions, take a skeptical attitude toward questionable arguments, evaluate evidence, formulate rational conclusions, and develop and refine participatory skills.

NEW YORK
Macmillan/McGraw-Hill TIMELINKS

Communities
Around the World

PROGRAM AUTHORS

James A. Banks
Kevin P. Colleary
Linda Greenow
Walter C. Parker
Emily M. Schell
Dinah Zike

CONTRIBUTORS

Raymond C. Jones
Irma M. Olmedo

 Macmillan/McGraw-Hill

PROGRAM AUTHORS

James A. Banks, Ph.D.
Kerry and Linda Killinger Professor
  of Diversity Studies
  and Director, Center for
  Multicultural Education
University of Washington
Seattle, Washington

Kevin P. Colleary, Ed.D.
Curriculum and Teaching Department
Graduate School of Education
Fordham University
New York, New York

Linda Greenow, Ph.D.
Associate Professor and Chair
Department of Geography
State University of New York at New Paltz
New Paltz, New York

Walter C. Parker, Ph.D.
Professor of Social Studies Education,
  Adjunct Professor of Political Science
University of Washington
Seattle, Washington

Emily M. Schell, Ed.D.
Visiting Professor, Teacher Education
San Diego State University
San Diego, California

Dinah Zike
Educational Consultant
Dinah-Mite Activities, Inc.
San Antonio, Texas

CONTRIBUTORS

Raymond C. Jones, Ph.D.
Director of Secondary Social Studies
  Education
Wake Forest University
Winston-Salem, North Carolina

Irma M. Olmedo
Associate Professor
University of Illinois-Chicago
College of Education
Chicago, Illinois

HISTORIANS/SCHOLARS

Manuel Chavez, Ph.D.
Associate Director, Center for
  Latin American & Caribbean Studies
Michigan State University
East Lansing, Michigan

Larry Dale, Ph.D.
Director, Northeast Arkansas Center for
  Economic Education
Arkansas State University
Jonesboro, Arkansas

Mac Dixon-Fyle, Ph.D.
Professor of History
DePauw University
Greencastle, Indiana

Brooks Green, Ph.D.
Professor of Geography
University of Central Arkansas
Conway, Arkansas

Jeffery D. Long, Ph.D.
Department Chair and Associate Professor
  of Religious Studies
Elizabethtown College
Elizabethtown, Pennsylvania

Peter N. Stearns, Ph.D.
Provost and Professor of History
George Mason University
Fairfax, Virginia

Jason R. Young, Ph.D.
Assistant Professor of History
State University of New York at Buffalo
Buffalo, New York

 Students with print disabilities may be eligible to obtain an accessible, audio version of the pupil edition of this textbook. Please call Recording for the Blind & Dyslexic at 1-800-221-4792 for complete information.

The McGraw-Hill Companies

Macmillan McGraw-Hill

MHID 0-02-152297-9

ISBN 978-0-02-152297-2

Printed in the United States of America

2 3 4 5 6 7 8 9 10   071/043   13 12 11 10 09

Communities Around the World
CONTENTS

Welcome to Your World   2

Unit 1   Mexico, a Land to the South   9

How does where people live affect how they live?

PEOPLE, PLACES, AND EVENTS   10

Lesson 1: The Land of Mexico   12

  Map and Globe Skills Understand Hemispheres   20

Lesson 2: The History of Mexico   22

  Chart and Graph Skills Use Time Lines   28

Lesson 3: Governing Mexico   30

Lesson 4: Mexico at Work   34

Lesson 5: Living in Mexico   40

Review and Assess/Test Preparation   46
The Big Idea Activities   48

Unit 2 Canada, Our Northern Neighbor 49

 How does a country change over time?

PEOPLE, PLACES, EVENTS	50
Lesson 1: The Land of Canada	52
Map and Globe Skills Understand Latitude and Longitude	60
Lesson 2: The History of Canada	62
Lesson 3: Governing Canada	68
Lesson 4: Canada at Work	72
Chart and Graph Skills Use Bar Graphs	78
Lesson 5: Living in Canada	80
Review and Assess/Test Preparation	86
The Big Idea Activities	88

Unit 3 South Africa, The Rainbow Nation 89

EXPLORE The Big Idea How do people change the place where they live?

PEOPLE, PLACES, AND EVENTS   90

Lesson 1: The Land of South Africa   92
   Map and Globe Skills Use Intermediate Directions   100

Lesson 2: The History of South Africa   102

Lesson 3: Governing South Africa   108

Lesson 4: South Africa at Work   112
   Chart and Graph Skills Use Line Graphs   118

Lesson 5: Living in South Africa   120

Review and Assess/Test Preparation   126
The Big Idea Activities   128

Unit 4   Italy, The Old and the New   129

EXPLORE The Big Idea   How do people in a country meet their needs?

PEOPLE, PLACES, AND EVENTS	130
Lesson 1: The Land of Italy	132
Map and Globe Skills Use Road Maps	140
Lesson 2: The History of Italy	142
Lesson 3: Governing Italy	148
Lesson 4: Italy at Work	152
Chart and Graph Skills Use Flow Charts	158
Lesson 5: Living in Italy	160
Review and Assess/Test Preparation	166
The Big Idea Activities	168

Unit 5 China, A Land of Contrasts 169

How do differences exist within and between communities?

PEOPLE, PLACES, AND EVENTS	170
Lesson 1: The Land of China	172
Map and Globe Skills Use Map Scales	180
Lesson 2: The History of China	182
Lesson 3: Governing China	188
Lesson 4: China at Work	192
Lesson 5: Living in China	198
Review and Assess/Test Preparation	206
The Big Idea Activities	208

Reference Section

Reading Skills   R2   Glossary   REF1

Geography Handbook   GH1   Index   REF5

Atlas   GH12   Credits   REF11

Maps

Mexico   4

Canada   5

South Africa   6

Italy   7

China   8

Mexico's Neighbors   13

Land in Mexico   14

Mexico's Top Export Partners, 2005   38

Natural Resources and Products in Mexico   37

Regions of Canada   54

French Exploration   64

English Exploration   65

Canada's Provinces and Territories   66

Canada's Natural Resources   74

Canada: Five Major Cities   83

South Africa   93

South Africa   101

South Africa's Resources   115

Northwest Italy   141

China: A Land of Many Regions   173

Largest Countries   175

Distances in China   181

Great Wall of China   184

Trade and Travel in Ancient China   193

United States: Political/Physical   GH12

World: Political   GH14

Skills and Features

Reading Skills

Main Idea and Details   R2

Sequence   R4

Summarize   R6

Cause and Effect   R8

Compare and Contrast   R10

Chart and Graph Skills

Use Time Lines   28

Use Bar Graphs   78

Use Line Graphs   118

Use Flow Charts   158

Map and Globe Skills

Understand Hemispheres   20

Understand Latitude and Longitude   60

Use Intermediate Directions   100

Use Road Maps   140

Use Map Scales   180

ix

Welcome to Your World

Countries You Will Learn About

CANADA

MEXICO

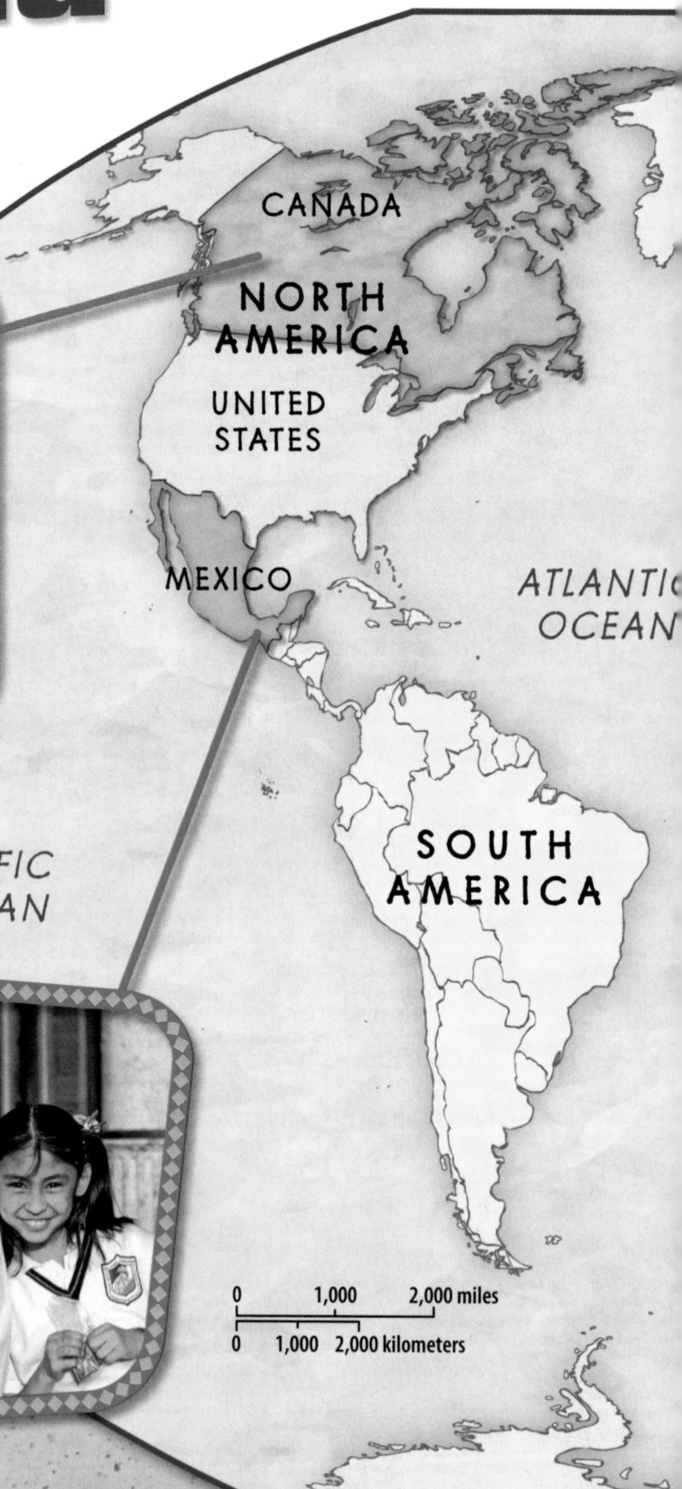

CANADA

NORTH AMERICA

UNITED STATES

MEXICO

ATLANTIC OCEAN

PACIFIC OCEAN

SOUTH AMERICA

0   1,000   2,000 miles

0   1,000   2,000 kilometers

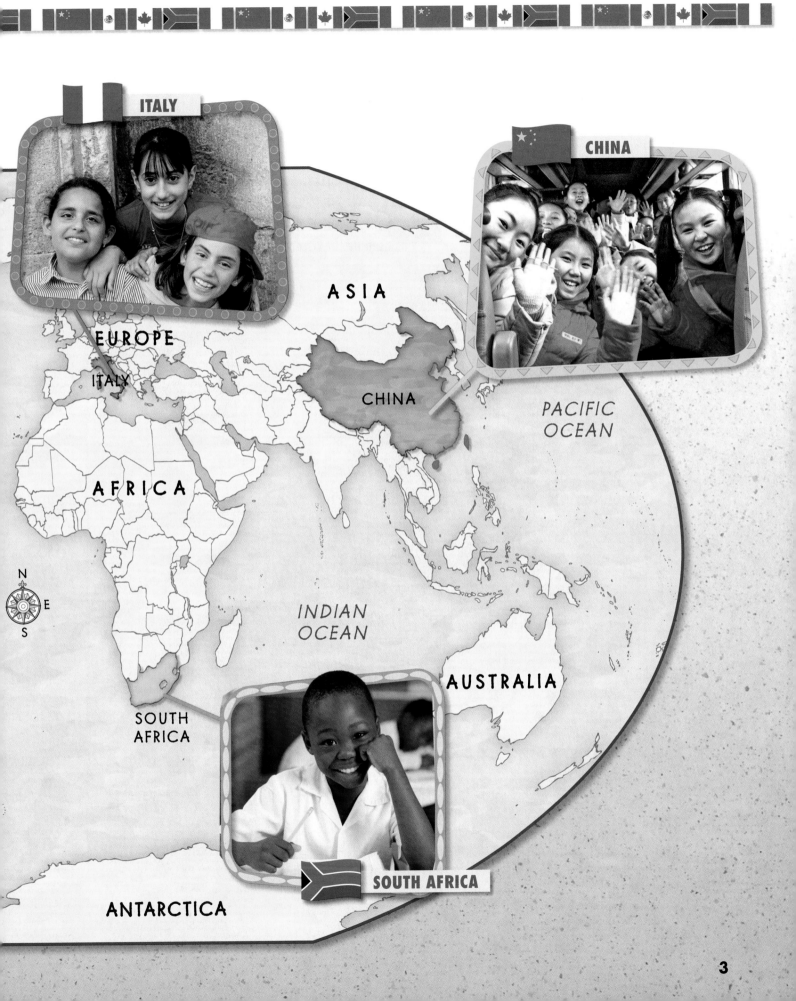

ITALY

CHINA

ASIA

EUROPE

ITALY

CHINA

PACIFIC
OCEAN

AFRICA

N
W · E
S

INDIAN
OCEAN

SOUTH
AFRICA

AUSTRALIA

SOUTH AFRICA

ANTARCTICA

3

Mexico: A Land to the South

Mexico is located on the continent of North America. It is the country directly south of the United States. In Unit 1 you will learn about some of Mexico's important people, places, and events.

Can you guess how this stone was used by the Aztec? ▶

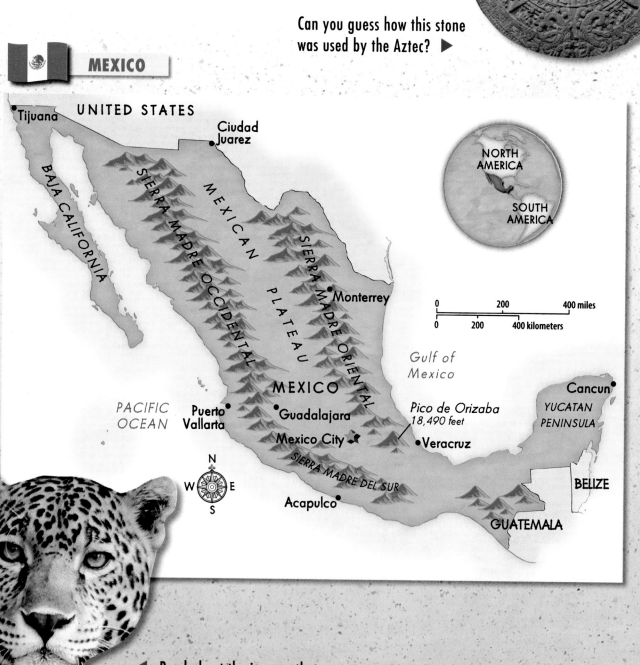

MEXICO

◀ Read about the jaguars that live in the rain forest.

Canada: Our Northern Neighbor

Canada is the largest country in land area in North America. It is also the second-largest country in the world! In Unit 2 you will read about the land and people that make up this great country.

▲ Where in Canada does the polar bear live?

CANADA

0   300   600 miles
0   300   600 kilometers

ARCTIC OCEAN

NORTH AMERICA

Mount Logan
19,550 feet

N
W   E
S

ATLANTIC OCEAN

PACIFIC OCEAN

ROCKY MOUNTAINS

CANADA

Hudson Bay

Vancouver

Quebec

Ottawa   Montreal

UNITED STATES

Toronto

How did the railroads change Canada's history? ▶

South Africa: The Rainbow Nation

South Africa is located on the continent of Africa. It is often called "The Rainbow Nation." Today, South Africa is a country made up of people from many diverse backgrounds. In Unit 3 you will read about important changes in this country.

What do rock paintings tell about early people? ▶

SOUTH AFRICA

ZIMBABWE

MOZAMBIQUE

EUROPE

AFRICA

0   100   200 miles
0   100   200 kilometers

BOTSWANA

Pretoria

Johannesburg

SWAZILAND

NAMIBIA

Kimberley

Njesuthi
11,181 feet

Bloemfontein

LESOTHO

DRAKENSBERG

Durban

N
W   E
S

SOUTH AFRICA

ATLANTIC
OCEAN

INDIAN
OCEAN

Cape Town

Port Elizabeth

Elephants are one of many kinds of animals that live in South Africa. ▶

Italy: The Old and the New

Italy is located on the continent of Europe. This country is easy to find on a map because of its shape. Many people think Italy looks like a tall boot with a high heel! Read more about Italy in Unit 4.

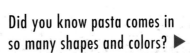

Did you know pasta comes in so many shapes and colors? ▶

ITALY

In which city will you see this beautiful church dome? ▼

China: A Land of Contrasts

China is located on the continent of Asia. It is the third-largest country in the world. Today, more than a billion people live in China! In Unit 5 you will learn how people's lives have changed over thousands of years.

The giant panda lives in China. ▶

CHINA

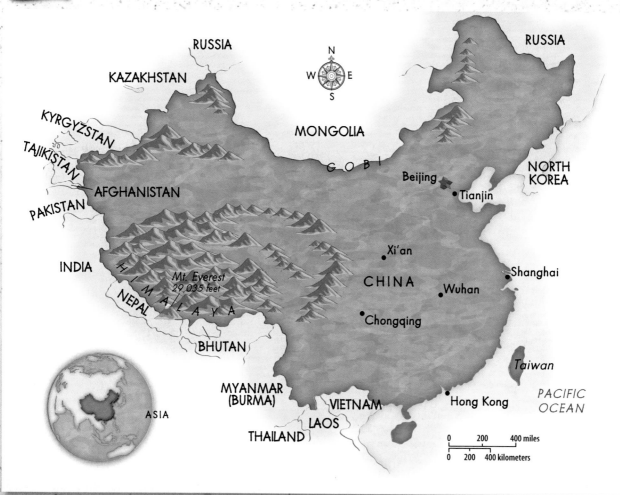

▼ The Great Wall of China is over 1,500 miles long.

8

EXPLORE The Big Idea

Essential Question

How does where people live affect how they live?

FOLDABLES™ Study Organizer

Main Idea and Details

Make and label a Concept Map Foldable before you read this unit. Write "Mexico" at the top. Label the three tabs **Geography**, **Government**, and **Economics**. Use the Foldable to organize information as you read about how Mexicans live.

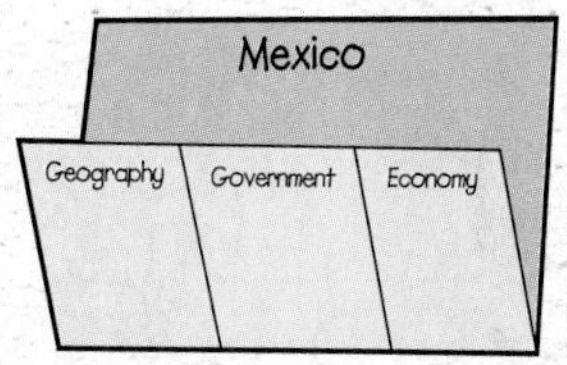

Mexico

| Geography | Government | Economy |

LOG ON

For more about Unit 1 go to
www.macmillanmh.com

Mexico's land formations vary from deserts to plains to mountains, such as these in Chihuahua, Mexico.

Mexico
A Land to the South

PEOPLE, PLACES, and EVENTS

Father Hidalgo

Historic church in Dolores Hidalgo

Cry of Dolores

1810

Father Hidalgo's cry for independence is repeated by the Mexican president every Independence Day in the town of Dolores.

In **1810 Father Miguel Hidalgo** rang the church bells in **Dolores** and called for independence from Spain.

Today you can visit the town of Dolores Hidalgo and see the church and Father Hidalgo's home.

LOG ON For more about People, Places, and Events, visit
www.macmillanmh.com

Frida Kahlo

Frida Kahlo Museum, Mexico City

Exhibition in Mexico City

1953

Many of Frida Kahlo's paintings were shown in her only solo exhibition in Mexico.

Frida Kahlo painted many pictures of herself and her family. She lived with her husband, the artist Diego Rivera, in **Mexico City**. Her last **exhibition, in 1953,** was a great success.

Today you can see her art in her house, now a museum.

Lesson 1

VOCABULARY

geography p. 14

land formations p. 14

plain p. 14

plateau p. 14

volcano p. 14

rain forest p. 15

climate p. 18

READING SKILLS

Main Idea and Details
Use the chart below to list the main ideas and details about Mexico's geography.

Main Idea	Details

New York Academic Content Standards
3.1, 3.2

The Land of MEXICO

Mexico has many beautiful beaches along its coast.

VISUAL PREVIEW

How does Mexico's land affect the people who live there?

A Mexico and the United States are neighbors.

B Mexico has different types of land, including deserts and volcanoes.

C Many kinds of plants and animals make their home in Mexico.

D The climate in Mexico affects how and where people live.

A FINDING MEXICO

Each fall millions of Monarch butterflies fly from the United States to central Mexico. They stay there until spring. Their flight path over Mexico leads them across its mountains, deserts, and plains. What a beautiful country to visit!

Where is Mexico in the world? Mexico is located on the continent of North America. Large bodies of water surround Mexico to the east and the west. If you look at the map, you can see that its shape is curved, like a giant fishhook!

Mexico's Neighbors

Mexico's neighbor to the north is the United States. Look at the map. Which states are the nearest to Mexico's northern border? To the south and east of Mexico are the countries of Guatemala and Belize.

Mexico's Neighbors

CALIFORNIA · ARIZONA · NEW MEXICO · UNITED STATES · TEXAS · Rio Grande · Gulf of California · Monterrey · MEXICO · Gulf of Mexico · PACIFIC OCEAN · Guadalajara · Mexico City ⊛ · Puebla · Balsas River · BELIZE · GUATEMALA · CENTRAL AMERICA

⊛ National capital
• Other city

Map Skill

LOCATION **What river is on the border of Mexico and the US.?**

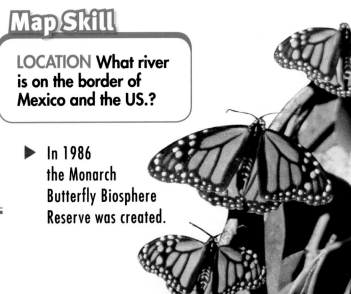

▶ In 1986 the Monarch Butterfly Biosphere Reserve was created.

QUICK CHECK

Main Idea and Details **Which countries are Mexico's neighbors?**

B TYPES OF LAND

Would you prefer to spend time in Mexico's mountains, deserts, or beaches? Many different types of land can be found in Mexico. Learning about Mexico's **geography** helps us understand how people live on its land. Geography is the study of land and water and the ways plants, people, and animals interact with them.

Mexico's Land Formations

Land formations are the shapes of Earth's surface. Mexico has high mountains, **plains**, and valleys. A plain is an area of flat land. It also has **plateaus**. A plateau is an area of flat land that is higher than the land around it.

The Plateau of Mexico is the largest land area in the country. It includes valleys, mountains, and **volcanoes**. A volcano is an opening in Earth's surface through which hot rocks and ash are forced out. The Plateau of Mexico is where most of Mexico's people live. Its largest cities, including the capital, Mexico City, are located there.

Deserts in the southwestern part of the United States spill over into Mexico. The deserts receive little rain and are very dry. Fewer people live in the deserts.

PACIFIC

Mountains
Plateaus
Plains
Valleys
Desert
Rainforest
National capital

QUICK CHECK

Main Idea and Details **What types of land formations can be found in the Plateau of Mexico?**

The Sierra mountains form a giant U-shape around the Plateau of Mexico. ▼

UNITED
STATES

SIERRA MADRE OCCIDENTAL

PLATEAU OF MEXICO

SIERRA MADRE ORIENTAL

OCEAN

MEXICO

Mexico City ⊛

SIERRA MADRE DEL SUR

Gulf of
Mexico

BELIZE

GUATEMALA

Mexico's rain forests are in the southern part of the country. Rain forests are thick forests that receive a large amount of rain.

N
W E
S

0   100   200 miles
0   100   200 kilometers

Sometimes people in Mexico City can see puffs of smoke from the volcano Popocatépetl. It is called "smoking mountain." It is so high that snow covers its top.

Map Skill

PLACE What is the land area in which Mexico's capital city is found?

C PLANTS AND ANIMALS

From cacti to spider monkeys, many different plants and animals make their homes in Mexico. In the mountain forests, trees such as the rosewood and walnut grow. There you may also see animals like bears, bobcats, and mountain lions.

Desert Life

What plants and animals live in the deserts of Mexico? Many kinds of cactus plants grow there. Because these plants store water in their stems, they can survive in a dry climate.

During the hot afternoons, desert animals stay in their cool homes. Prairie dogs live in underground burrows, while snakes and lizards live under rocks. Some insects and birds make their homes in the cactus plants. When the desert cools off at night, it comes alive with the sights and sounds of these different creatures.

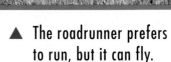

▲ The roadrunner prefers to run, but it can fly.

▼ The Mexican Red Knee Tarantula is brightly colored.

▼ The Saguaro cactus can grow as tall as 50 feet!

The Rain Forests of Mexico

The seasons do not change in the rain forest. The warm temperature stays about the same all year round. This helps the trees grow very tall. The tallest rain forest tree is more than 165 feet high. The plants and animals help each other survive in the rain forests. Many insects and birds make their homes in its trees.

Insects, birds, snakes, and frogs all live in Mexico's rain forests. Mammals in the rain forest include tiny bats, spider monkeys, and jaguars. The jaguar is the largest wild cat in North America. When people destroy the Mexican rain forests, they also endanger the many animals who live there—even the mighty jaguar.

▲ The quetzal is known for its beautiful colors.

▼ Ancient Mexican people believed the jaguar was a god.

QUICK CHECK

Main Idea and Details **Why can cactus plants survive in the desert?**

Tall trees, thick shrubs, and climbing vines grow in rain forests.

▼ Orchids grow in the rain forest's warm, wet climate.

LIVING IN DIFFERENT CLIMATES

The **climate** is different depending on which area of Mexico you are in. Climate is the pattern of weather in a place over many years. People adapt their lives and work according to the climate.

Making It in the Desert

The desert climate is very hot, and therefore there is not enough water to grow crops. To farm the dry land, farmers in villages and towns use pipes or ditches to bring in water from other areas. They may also farm in the high mountains where there is some rain. Fewer people live in Mexico's desert areas because it is hard to work and live there. During the winter months, it is often cold at night, while in the summer it is very hot.

The Plateau of Mexico

The northern part of the Plateau of Mexico gets little rain, so it is dry. The southern part gets more rain, so farmers grow more crops there. The beautiful Valley of Mexico, the busy center of Mexican life, is found in the southern part of Mexico. People who live here spend a lot of time outdoors because of the mild weather.

▲ Adobe houses are found in desert areas. Adobe walls keep homes cool in the summer.

▼ A Mexican woman harvests chili peppers.

▶ Local workers process coffee beans. Coffee is grown in Mexico's rain forests.

Resources of the Rain Forest

Some plants and trees can only grow in the climate of the rain forest. They can be found just in this area. There are many unique products that come from the rain forests. Plants are used to make foods and medicines. Trees from the rain forest provide timber for furniture and buildings. However, cutting down too many trees can hurt the soil, making it difficult for trees and other plants to grow. People need to both enjoy and protect the resources of the rain forests.

People who live in the rain forest get their food by hunting, fishing, and gathering plants to eat. These Mexican people know a lot about the rain forest's plants and animals. Some had ancestors who lived in the region hundreds of years ago.

QUICK CHECK

Main Idea and Details **What is the climate like in Mexico's deserts?**

Check Understanding

1. **VOCABULARY** Write one sentence for each vocabulary word below.
   geography   plateau
   land formation   rain forest

2. **READING SKILL Main Idea and Details** Use the chart from page 12 to write a paragraph about the geography of Mexico.

Main Idea	Details

3. **Write About It** How do Mexicans live in the different areas of the country?

Map and Globe Skills
Understanding Hemispheres

VOCABULARY

sphere

hemisphere

prime meridian

equator

Today people come to Mexico from all over the world. You can find these different places on a globe, a model of Earth. A globe is a **sphere**. It is round, like a ball. You can see only half of a globe at a time. The part of the globe you see is called a **hemisphere**, which means "half of a sphere."

Learn It

We can divide Earth into hemispheres from top to bottom or around the middle.

W   E

- The **prime meridian** is an imaginary line that runs from the North Pole to the South Pole through Greenwich, England. Places east of this line are in the Eastern Hemisphere. Places west of this line are in the Western Hemisphere.

N

S

- The **equator** is an imaginary line around Earth halfway between the North Pole and the South Pole. Any place north of this line is in the Northern Hemisphere. Any place south of this line is in the Southern Hemisphere.

- A continent can be in more than one hemisphere.

Four Hemispheres

Western Hemisphere

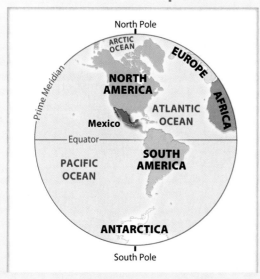

Eastern Hemisphere

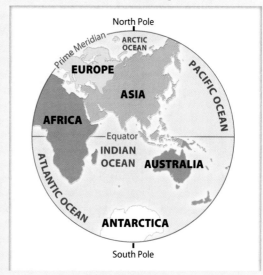

Northern Hemisphere

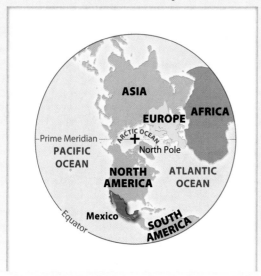

Southern Hemisphere

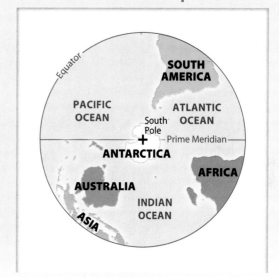

Try It

Look at the maps to answer the questions.

- What are the four hemispheres?

- Which hemisphere on the map is south of the equator?

Apply It

- Find Mexico on two of the maps. On which continent is Mexico?

- In which hemispheres is Mexico?

Lesson 2

VOCABULARY

prehistoric p. 23

civilization p .23

explorer p. 24

hacienda p. 25

republic p. 26

revolution p. 27

READING SKILLS

Main Ideas and Details
Use the chart below to list the main ideas and details about Mexico's history.

Main Idea	Details

New York Academic Content Standards

2.1, 2.2, 2.3, 2.4, 3.1, 4.1, 5.1

THE HISTORY OF MEXICO

Mayan palaces and temples hint at the grandness of Mayan culture.

 VISUAL PREVIEW

How has Mexico changed because of historical events?

A The Aztec created their civilization mostly in the Valley of Mexico.

B The Spanish were drawn to Mexico's resources of gold and silver.

C Mexicans fought and won their independence from Spain.

Ⓐ FOUNDING MEXICO

Corn has been important to Mexicans throughout their history. The Aztec showed corn many pieces of art. They also used it to make a pancake called a tortilla. Tortillas are still eaten today.

In **prehistoric** times, before people wrote down history, hunters from the north arrived in Mexico. They learned to grow crops such as beans and corn. As farmers, they settled in villages and built Mexico's first **civilizations**, or developed communities.

Civilizations of the Past

One of the first civilizations were the Maya. The Maya built houses, temples, and pyramids in southern Mexico. Mayan people still live in southern Mexico today.

The Aztec, another early civilization, founded many cities and towns, especially in the Valley of Mexico. The Aztec were great warriors who conquered other people in Mexico. In A.D. 1325 the Aztec built their capital, Tenochtitlán, on an island in the middle of a beautiful lake. This is where Mexico City is located today.

The Aztec Calendar Stone was used in ceremonies. The Aztec calendar had 365 days. ▼

QUICK CHECK

Main Ideas and Details **Who were two ancient Mexican peoples?**

B SPANISH RULE

In 1519 Hernán Cortés, the Spanish **explorer**, and his soldiers arrived by ship on the eastern coast of Mexico. An explorer goes to a place to find out about it. Life was to change greatly for the Aztec people.

The Spanish Conquest

Two years later, Cortés conquered the Aztec. The Spanish destroyed Tenochtitlán, and built Mexico City in its place. Spain ruled Mexico for the next 300 years. The native people had to change their religion and become Christians, like the Spanish. They were also forced to pay a special tax to Spain. The Spanish king did allow the native people to speak their own language.

Some Aztec towns had plazas with temple pyramids. What else can you tell about Aztec life from the picture below?

PEOPLE

Moctezuma II was the Aztec ruler when the Spanish came to Mexico. He tried to get the Spanish to leave Mexico.

Moctezuma II

Spanish soldiers wore armor and carried guns. They rode on horses.

After the conquest, many Spanish people moved to Mexico. They brought a new culture, including the Spanish language. They brought animals never seen in Mexico, such as horses, donkeys, and oxen. They introduced the native people to the wheel, to crops such as sugarcane, and to new crafts.

Discovery of Gold and Silver

The Spanish found gold and silver in Mexico. These riches attracted more settlers from Spain, and many mines were created. To feed and clothe the people in these new communities, they built large estates called **haciendas**. The native people had to live and work on these haciendas whenever needed. The native people remained poor, but the mines made Spain rich.

▼ Silver was used to make Spanish coins.

QUICK CHECK

Main Idea and Details What new animals did Spain introduce to Mexico?

MEXICAN INDEPENDENCE

In 1776 the American War of Independence had begun. Many Mexicans also wanted their freedom. The spirit of independence was in the air.

Mexican War of Independence

Many Mexicans felt that the Spanish were treating them unfairly. Early in the morning of September 16, 1810, Father Miguel Hidalgo made history with a speech in the small town of Dolores. Father Hidalgo's words, known as the "Cry of Dolores," called for the people to rise up and fight for their freedom from the Spanish. It was the beginning of the Mexican War of Independence.

Although Spain tried to stop them, in 1821 Mexico became independent. In 1824 Mexico became a **republic**, a nation without a king or queen. A period of confusion followed. Many different presidents and governments ruled the country over the next several years.

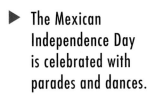
▲ There are monuments to Father Hidalgo all over Mexico. This one is in Mexico City.

► The Mexican Independence Day is celebrated with parades and dances.

War With the United States

In 1836 American settlers in Texas, then part of Mexico, fought for Texas to be independent. Mexican troops defeated them at the Battle of the Alamo in Texas. Both Mexico and the United States continued to claim Texas. In 1846 the United States declared war on Mexico. When this war ended in 1848, Mexico lost its northern territories to the United States. Today this land makes up the states of California, Nevada, and Utah, as well as parts of other states.

The Revolution of 1910

Mexico's problems continued. A few wealthy families owned most of the land, while the rest of the people were very poor. People wanted change. In 1910 leaders of the Mexican Revolution led attacks across the country. A **revolution** is the overthrowing of a government. When the Mexican Revolution ended in 1920, Mexico was a changed nation. It was ready to improve the life of its people.

▲ Mexican troops stormed the Alamo, a fortress in Texas.

Check Understanding

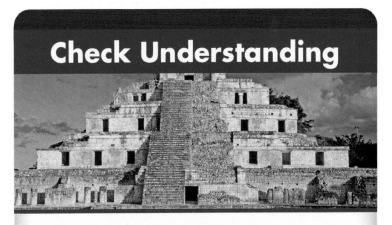

1. **VOCABULARY** Write one sentence for each vocabulary word below.

   prehistoric   civilization

   republic   hacienda

2. **READING SKILL Main Idea and Details** Use the chart from page 22 to write a paragraph about new people arriving in Mexico.

Main Idea	Details

3. **Write About It** How did life change in Mexico after the Spanish conquest?

QUICK CHECK

Main Idea and Details What was life in Mexico like after the country became a republic?

Chart and Graph Skills

Use Time Lines

VOCABULARY

time line

century

You have read about events in Mexico's past. It is not always easy to remember what happened first, next, and last. A **time line** tells the order of important events. Looking at a time line tells you when a certain event took place. Learning to use time lines will help you better understand events in the past.

Learn It

Follow these steps, and look at the time line below as you read.

- Look at the dates on the time line. Time lines are divided to show time periods, such as years or centuries. A **century** is 100 years. This time line covers the centuries between 1300 and 1900.

- Look at the order of events. Events are listed in time order from left to right. An event to the left of another event took place earlier.

- Use the dates to tell the number of years between events. Subtract the date of the earlier event from the date of the later event.

Mexico's History

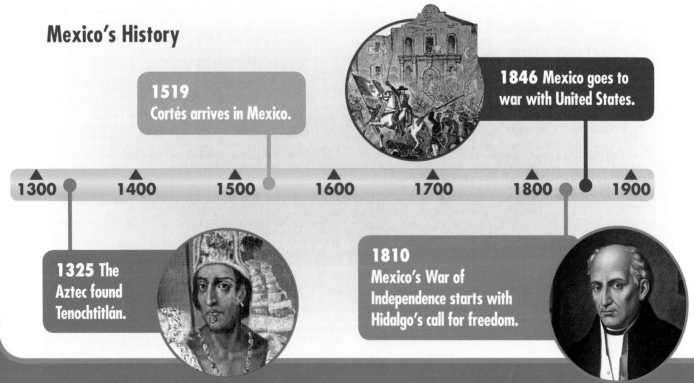

1519 Cortés arrives in Mexico.

1846 Mexico goes to war with United States.

1300 1400 1500 1600 1700 1800 1900

1325 The Aztec found Tenochtitlán.

1810 Mexico's War of Independence starts with Hidalgo's call for freedom.

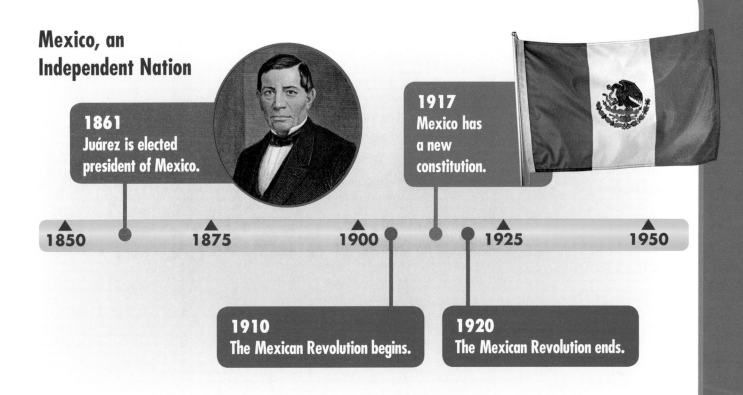

Mexico, an Independent Nation

1861
Juárez is elected president of Mexico.

1917
Mexico has a new constitution.

1850   1875   1900   1925   1950

1910
The Mexican Revolution begins.

1920
The Mexican Revolution ends.

Try It

Use the time line above to answer the questions.

- What period of time does this time line cover?

- How many years does this time line cover?

- What happened in 1917?

- Which happened last—Juárez was elected president, or the Mexican Revolution began?

Apply It

- Make a time line of your own life.

- Divide your time line into years.

- Decide on five important events to include on your time line.

VOCABULARY

democracy p. 31

constitution p. 31

legislative branch p. 32

executive branch p. 32

judicial branch p. 32

READING SKILLS

Main Idea and Details
Use the chart below to list the main ideas and details about Mexico's government.

Main Idea	Details

New York Academic Content Standards
2.2, 2.3, 5.1, 5.2, 5.3

GOVERNING MEXICO

The president of Mexico works in the National Palace in Mexico City. The current palace was built in 1693.

VISUAL PREVIEW

How does Mexico's government serve its people?

A Mexico is a democracy like the United States.

B Mexico has a national government and state governments.

A THE UNITED MEXICAN STATES

Mexico's flag was first used after its War of Independence in 1821. Its three colors—red, white and green—have stood for different things over time. What do you think they symbolize?

Mexico's official name is the United Mexican States. Does this name remind you of the name of another country? If you guessed the United States of America, you are correct! Mexico and the United States have similar governments. Like the United States, Mexico is a **democracy**. A democracy is a country whose government is run by its people.

▲ Mexico's coat of arms shows an eagle on a cactus. What is in its beak?

QUICK CHECK

Main Ideas and Details In what year was Mexico's flag first used?

Citizenship

A New Constitution

In 1916 people came together to write a **constitution** for Mexico. A constitution is a document containing the laws of a government. The new constitution took effect in 1917. This important group of laws guarantees the rights and freedoms of the Mexican people. It also explains the rules for organizing the Mexican government.

Write About It What was the purpose of writing the Mexican constitution?

Ⓑ MEXICO'S GOVERNMENT

Like the United States, Mexico has national and state governments. Each state in Mexico has a governor and legislature, which are elected by the citizens, and its own constitution. Who is the governor of your state? Do you know when he or she was elected?

National Government

The Mexican Constitution of 1917 divided the national government into three branches or parts: the **legislative branch** writes new laws; the **executive branch** carries out the laws; and the **judicial branch** decides if the laws are fair and follow the constitution. How are the governments of the United States and Mexico alike and different? Read the chart below.

Governments of Mexico and the United States

Mexico	United States
National government has three branches: legislative, executive, judicial	National government has three branches: legislative, executive, judicial
There are 31 states.	There are 50 states.
National constitution	National constitution
Congress with a Senate and Chamber of Deputies	Congress with a Senate and House of Representatives
Supreme Court is highest court in land	Supreme Court is highest court in land
President serves for one term that lasts six years. There is no vice-president.	President can serve for two terms. Each term lasts four years. There is a vice-president.

Today, more Mexicans read and write than before 1917. This is because more children go to school.

Children's Rights in Mexico

In Mexico children also get involved. On July 6, 1997, almost four million boys and girls in Mexico voted on the rights that were important to them. The one that received the most votes was the right to have a school. Next, boys and girls voted to live in a place where the air, water, and land were clean. Other rights included the right to eat healthy foods and the right to not work before the legal working age. What are some rights that you would add to this list?

QUICK CHECK

Main Idea and Details **How is power divided in Mexico's national government?**

Check Understanding

1. **VOCABULARY** Write a short paragraph about Mexico's government using the vocabulary words below.
   legislative branch   executive branch
   judicial branch   democracy

2. **READING SKILL** Main Ideas and Details Use the chart from page 30 to write a paragraph about the organization of Mexico's government.

Main Idea	Details

EXPLORE The Big Idea

3. **Write About It** What parts of Mexico's government are similar to the United States?

Mexico at Work

VOCABULARY

natural resource p. 36

mineral p. 36

factory p. 38

export p. 38

import p. 38

economy p. 39

READING SKILLS

Main Idea and Details
Use the chart below to list the main idea and details about Mexico's economy.

Main Idea	Details

New York Academic Content Standards
3.1, 3.2, 4.1, 4.2

Many fruits and vegetables are grown and sold in Mexico. People can buy them at outdoor markets such as this one.

VISUAL PREVIEW

How has work in Mexico changed over time?

A Farming continues to be important in Mexico.

B People use Mexico's natural resources to make products.

C Today, many Mexicans work in factories and other industries.

Ⓐ MEXICO'S CROPS

Since ancient times, corn and beans have been important crops in Mexico. People in Mexico have been harvesting corn for thousands of years!

In Mexico today, farmers still grow corn and beans. Other crops, such as coffee and cotton, are also produced on their farms. Cows, chickens, and sheep are raised around the country.

Mexico's Farms

You learned about the large estates called haciendas, where native groups worked for Spanish landowners. This continued until the early 1900s. The Constitution of 1917 changed this. New laws divided many estates into smaller portions of land and gave them to Mexico's workers. Under this new system, communities owned land too. Some farmers in these communities worked the land together and shared the crops they grow.

Today in Mexico there is a mix of community farms, small family farms, and large estates. More modern ways to farm have been introduced.

QUICK CHECK

Main Idea and Details
What are the different kinds of farms found in Mexico today?

▶ A goatherd leads goats through a field to find food.

A WEALTH OF RESOURCES

▲ These handcrafted earrings are made from silver.

Mexico has many **natural resources**, which are materials found in nature that people use. Examples of natural resources include oil, silver, and crops. People use these resources to make products, such as jewelry and clothing. Take a look at the map to see where some natural resources and products are found.

Where to Farm?

It is hard to grow crops in Mexico because it has many mountains and not much rain. People farm only a small part of Mexico's land. The best farmland in Mexico is in the southern part of the Plateau of Mexico, which has a mild climate, rain, and rich land. There, crops such as cotton, beans, and corn are grown. The hot, rainy areas of Mexico are good for growing cacao, the plant from which chocolate is made.

Heat and Coins

The Spanish became rich from Mexico's silver. Silver is a **mineral**, a natural resource that is not a plant or animal. More silver is mined in Mexico than anywhere else in the world. Another important mineral resource produced in Mexico is oil. People use this oil to heat their homes and other buildings.

PLACES

The Spanish discovered silver near this city more than 450 years ago! This discovery led to a major mining rush and an increase in Spanish settlers. You can still see its most important mine today.

Zacatecas, Mexico

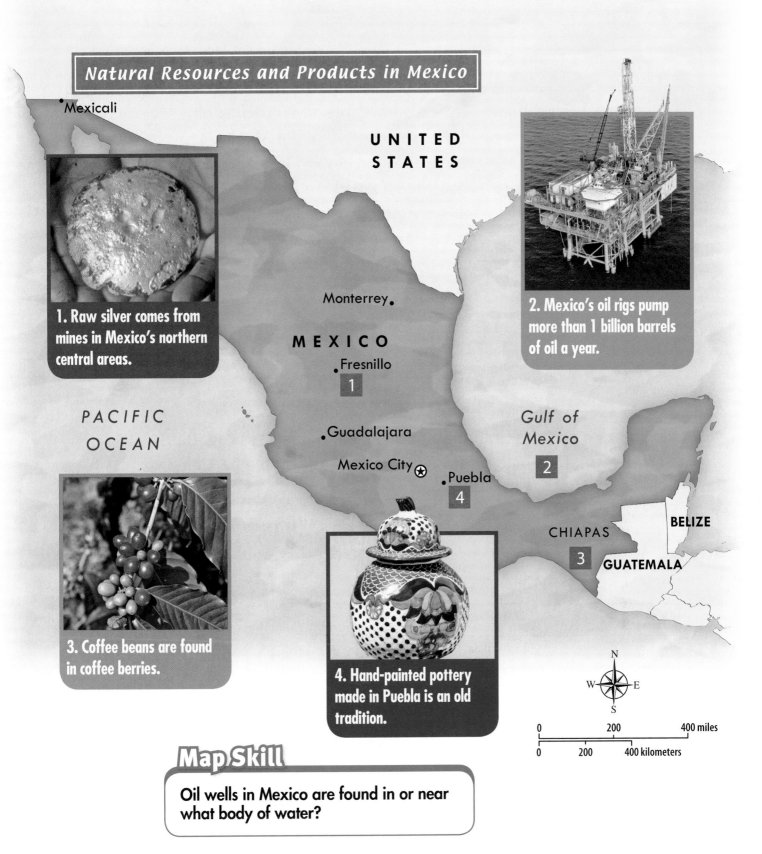

Natural Resources and Products in Mexico

Mexicali

UNITED STATES

Monterrey

MEXICO

Fresnillo

1. Raw silver comes from mines in Mexico's northern central areas.

PACIFIC OCEAN

Guadalajara

Mexico City

Puebla

4

Gulf of Mexico

2. Mexico's oil rigs pump more than 1 billion barrels of oil a year.

2

CHIAPAS

BELIZE

3

GUATEMALA

3. Coffee beans are found in coffee berries.

4. Hand-painted pottery made in Puebla is an old tradition.

N
W E
S

| 0 | 200 | 400 miles |
| 0 | 200 | 400 kilometers |

Map Skill

Oil wells in Mexico are found in or near what body of water?

QUICK CHECK

Main Idea and Details **Why is it easier for Mexican farmers to grow crops in the southern part of the Plateau of Mexico?**

Today, many Mexicans have jobs in **factories**, or places where products are made. Most of Mexico's factories are located in or near Mexico City. They make about half of all the products made in Mexico! Mexico **exports** many of these products, which means it sends them to other countries to be sold. It also **imports**, or buys, many products from other countries.

DataGraphic
Trading Partners

Mexico and the United States do a lot of business together! The graphics below show Mexico's major trading partners.

Mexico's Top Import Partners, 2005

Country	Amount
United States	$118.5 billion
China	$17.8 billion
Japan	$13.1 billion

Source: U.S. Department of State, 2007

Mexico's Top Export Partners, 2005

CANADA

$4.3 billion

UNITED STATES

$181.9 billion

MEXICO

Think About Imports and Exports

1. How many billions of dollars worth of goods does Mexico export to the United States?

2. How much more does Mexico import from China than Japan?

Helping the Economy

Many Mexicans have jobs in businesses that help people. Some work with the people who visit Mexico. Others have jobs in schools, parks, banks, and stores. Their work helps Mexico's **economy**, which is the way a country produces and uses its goods, natural resources, and services.

A Growing Business

Millions of people visit Mexico every year. They come to see ancient cities, enjoy the busy life in Mexico City, and relax on Mexico's beaches. They stay in hotels and eat in restaurants. Visitors buy Mexican crafts. Different places in the country specialize in making craft products, such as pottery, masks, baskets, and silver jewelry. Some craftsmen are continuing ancient native or Spanish traditions. Others are creating new styles.

▲ The city of Oaxaca is known for its hand-painted wooden animals.

QUICK CHECK

Main Idea and Details **What are common jobs in Mexico today?**

Mexico's beaches are a popular vacation spot.

Check Understanding

1. **VOCABULARY** Write one sentence for each vocabulary word below.

   export   natural resources

   factory   mineral

2. **READING SKILL Main Idea and Details** Use the chart from page 34 to write a paragraph about the economy of Mexico.

Main Idea	Details

3. **Write About It** How does Mexico's geography affect its economy?

Lesson 5

VOCABULARY

immigrant p. 41

pollution p. 41

plaza p. 43

culture p. 44

fiesta p. 45

READING SKILLS

Main Ideas and Details
Use the chart below to list the main ideas and details about Mexico City.

Main Idea	Details

New York Academic Content Standards
2.1, 2.3, 2.4, 3.1

LIVING IN MEXICO

The golden angel of the Monument to Independence can be seen at the Reforma Boulevard, a major avenue in Mexico City.

VISUAL PREVIEW

What is life like in Mexico City?

A Mexico City, the country's capital, is the center of life in Mexico.

B Many famous buildings are located in Mexico City.

C Mexico City has an exciting cultural life.

A LIFE IN A MEXICAN CITY

Did you know that Mexico City is one of the largest cities in the world? Built on the same site as the Aztec capital, it is still the heart of the nation.

Today more people live in Mexico City and the suburbs around it than in any other Mexican city. Other important cities in the Plateau of Mexico are Puebla, one of Mexico's oldest cities, and Guadalajara. Although some Mexicans still live in small villages, most live in cities and large towns.

Capital City

Mexico City, the capital, is a busy place to live and work. It is the center of life in Mexico. Many businesses, museums, and universities are found there. Some people in Mexico City are **immigrants**, people who come from one country to live in another. They moved from countries in Europe, Asia, and the Middle East. Because so many people live and work in this city, it is crowded and has a lot of traffic. This has created a problem with **pollution**, where the air is made dirty from harmful materials.

A girl in traditional dress dances in Mexico City. ▼

QUICK CHECK

Main Idea and Details Why is Mexico City a center of Mexican life?

A CITY OF MANY SIGHTS

▲ In front of Chapultepec Castle is a monument to six young soldiers who died protecting the castle during the war with the United States.

Every day, people from all over the world arrive at Mexico City's airport. They can't wait to see its beautiful sights. What would you plan to see in your tour of this exciting city?

Parks and Lakes

The largest park in Mexico City is Chapultepec Park. It includes the former home to Mexican presidents, Chapultepec Castle. You can also see rare native artifacts in the National Museum of Anthropology, located in the park. Many boats travel along the canals dug by the Aztecs and pass through the "Floating Gardens."

▼ The Aztec built islands in the canals and grew flowers and fruits on them. These became known as the "Floating Gardens."

Going Downtown

You can learn about all the time periods in Mexico's history with a visit to one place! The huge public square called the Zócalo is located in downtown Mexico City. There you can see Spanish and modern buildings, standing side by side. There are even parts of the ancient Aztec temple that survived.

The official name of the Zócalo is Constitution Plaza. A **plaza** is an open public square in a town or city. Many important buildings surround this plaza. One is the Metropolitan Cathedral, Mexico's largest church, that was finished in 1737. It is located near the place where a huge Aztec pyramid, Templo Mayor, once stood. What is left of this Aztec temple was discovered and can now be seen in an outdoor museum called the Main Temple. The beautiful National Palace is also found in the plaza.

▲ The Metropolitan Cathedral and National Palace are both in the Constitution Plaza.

EVENT

A major earthquake struck Mexico City in 1985. Thousands of people died, and about 400 buildings collapsed. Many other buildings were damaged.

Earthquake in Mexico City

QUICK CHECK

Main Idea and Details **What is the name of the largest park in Mexico City?**

THE CULTURE IN MEXICO CITY

You can enjoy a lot of Mexico's culture in Mexico City. **Culture** is a way of life shared by a group of people. It includes anything that makes a country special, such as its language, art, dance, food, sports, and holidays.

The Arts in Mexico City

Mexicans love dancing. A famous group of Mexican dancers, the Ballet Folklórico de Mexico, performs at the Bellas Artes Palace in downtown Mexico City. Their dancing mixes lively music with traditional folkdances.

Colorful art is another part of Mexican culture. You read about a famous artist, Frida Kahlo, on page 11. Her husband, Diego Rivera, painted large wall paintings called murals. He loved to paint scenes of Mexican life. What is happening below in the mural by Diego Rivera?

Primary Sources

"The earliest memory I have is that I was drawing."

"I was a dynamo of energy. . . For days on end I painted from early dawn til past midnight."

From his autobiography, *My Art, My Life*
Diego Rivera

Write About It Write a sentence that describes your favorite activity.

This is a detail of a mural called "Totonac Civilization," located in the National Palace. ▼

Mexicans Celebrate

Walk through Mexico City and you will see groups of musicians playing violins, guitars, and horns. These bands are called mariachis. Music is also played at Mexican celebrations. At Mexican parties called **fiestas** there is dancing, singing and wonderful food.

"Fiestas Patrias"

One of Mexico City's greatest fiestas takes place on the most important national holiday—Independence Day. Mexicans celebrate their independence from Spain on two days, September 15 and 16. They call this the "Fiestas Patrias." *Patria* means "country" in Spanish. What does the holiday's Spanish name mean?

QUICK CHECK

Main Idea and Details **What is culture?**

▲ Mariachi bands often perform at marriages and festivals.

Check Understanding

1. **VOCABULARY** Write a short letter to a friend about a visit to Mexico City. Use the vocabulary words below.

   immigrant   **plaza**

   pollution   **fiesta**

2. **READING SKILL** Main Ideas and Details Use the chart from page 40 to write a paragraph about life in Mexico City.

Main Idea	Details

 3. **Write About It** What types of things are there to do for people living in Mexico City?

Unit 1 Review

Vocabulary

Number a paper from 1 to 3. Beside each number write the word from the list below that matches the number.

democracy   republic   export

1. a system of government in which people elect their leaders
2. to send goods out of a country to be sold
3. a nation without a king or queen

Comprehension and Critical Thinking

4. How is the climate in the northern and southern parts of Mexico's central plateau different?

5. How did the discover of gold and silver affect life in Mexico?

6. Reading Skills What is one way that Mexico's economy is changing?

7. Critical Thinking Why do so many people come to Mexico City to live?

Skill

Time Line

Study the time line. Then write a complete sentence to answer each question.

8. When did workers begin to build the Metropolitan Cathedral?

9. Did an earthquake strike Mexico City before or after the Bellas Artes was built?

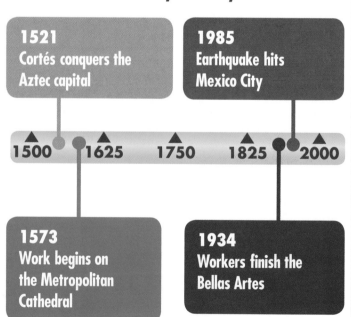

Mexico City History

1521 Cortés conquers the Aztec capital

1985 Earthquake hits Mexico City

1500   1625   1750   1825   2000

1573 Work begins on the Metropolitan Cathedral

1934 Workers finish the Bellas Artes

New York English Language Arts Test Preparation

Directions

Read this article about making guacamole. Then answer questions 1 and 2.

Ingredients

- 2 large ripe avocados
- 1 small red onion, chopped
- 2 tbsp lime juice
- 1 tomato, seeded and chopped
- 1 jalapeno pepper, seeded and chopped
- 1 tsp ground cumin
- 1/4 cup chopped cilantro
- 1/2 tsp salt

Cooking Instructions

1. Cut the avocados in half, remove the pit, and peel them. If they are ripe, the peel should come off easily. Dice the avocado flesh, and dump into a bowl.

2. Add the remaining ingredients. Toss to combine without mashing.

3. Serve with tortilla chips for dipping.

---

1 What should you do **before** peeling the avocado?

A mash the avocado

B chop the tomato

C remove the pit

D dice the avocado

2 What is the **last** step of the recipe?

A peel the avocados

B serve with chips

C chop the tomato

D dump the avocados in a bowl

Activities

How does where people live affect how they live?

Write About the Big Idea

Descriptive Paragraph

Think about what you have read about the land and people of Mexico in Unit 1. Then complete the Foldable with the main ideas and details from the lessons. Once you have completed this Foldable, use it to help you write a paragraph that answers the Big Idea question "How does where people live affect how they live?" Be sure to begin with a sentence that tells the main idea of your paragraph. Then write three or four sentences about the details on your chart. End with a sentence that sums up the main idea of thought of your paragraph.

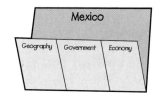

Make a Travel Poster

Work in small groups to make a travel poster about Mexico. Your travel poster should make people want to visit this exciting country. Use information you learned in Unit 1 about life in Mexico for your poster. Here's how to make your travel poster.

1. Collect materials for your poster: drawing paper, pencils, pens, markers, crayons, paint.

2. Think of a title for your poster.

3. Work together to write three sentences that answer this question: Why is Mexico a fun country to visit?

4. Each student in the group should write one of the answers on your poster.

5. Draw pictures about life in Mexico.

6. Put your poster on a special class bulletin board. Then talk about your poster with your classmates.

Unit 2

EXPLORE
The
Big
Idea

Essential Question
How does a country
change over time?

FOLDABLES™
Study Organizer

Sequence
Make and label an
Accordion Foldable with
**Before 1600, 1600s–1800s,
1900s,** and **Today.** Use this Foldable
to take notes on important dates and
changes in Canadian history and life.

Today

1900s

1600s–
1800s

Before
1600

LOG
ON

For more about this unit go to
www.macmillanmh.com

Canada is a big, beautiful country
that is located to the north
of the United States.

Canada, Our Northern Neighbor

PEOPLE, PLACES, AND EVENTS

St. Lawrence River

Samuel de Champlain

The French settle Quebec

1608
The city of Quebec was the first French settlement in Canada. When the French arrived, they met many native Canadians.

French explorer **Samuel de Champlain** established a fur-trading post along the **St. Lawrence River** in 1608. The new city became known as **Quebec**.

Today almost half a million people live in the city of Quebec.

LOG ON For more about People, Places, and Events, visit
www.macmillanmh.com

Lucy Maud Montgomery

Prince Edward Island

Montgomery wrote *Anne of Green Gables*

1908

Montgomery was a famous Canadian children's writer. She lived for a time in this large house in Leaskdale, a town near Toronto. She wrote many of her books here.

Lucy Maud Montgomery was born in 1874 on **Prince Edward Island**. After teaching school, she began to write books.

Today many children read her most famous novel, ***Anne of Green Gables***. It is based on her childhood memories.

The Land OF Canada

Goats live in the mountains of Canada.

VOCABULARY

coastline p. 53

region p. 54

lowland p. 54

tundra p. 56

prairie p. 58

READING SKILL

Main Idea and Details
Use the chart below to list facts about Canada's geography.

Main Idea	Details

New York Academic Content Standards
3.1, 3.2

VISUAL PREVIEW

What is life like in the different regions of Canada?

A Different regions make up the geography of Canada.

B In the lowlands, life and work change with the seasons.

C Few people live in the year-round cold of the frozen tundra.

D Canada's west has plains, prairies, and mountains.

A CANADA'S LAND

Tall mountains and flat prairies are just two types of land you can find in Canada. There is so much to know about the geography of Canada!

Canada is the largest country in North America. It is also the second-largest country in the world. Although Canada is a little bigger than the United States, many fewer people live there. You will find out why in this lesson.

▲ When driving in Canada, watch out for moose!

Water and Land

Oceans surround Canada on the east, west, and north. Look at the map on the next page and trace the **coastline** of Canada with your finger. A coastline is land along an ocean. Canada's coastline is 151,488 miles long!

Canada has very tall, jagged mountains in the west and lower, more rounded mountains in the east. The land in the middle of the country is good for farming. There are also forests and many rivers and lakes.

QUICK CHECK

Main Idea and Details **What is the difference between Canada's mountains in the east and west?**

The Great Lakes contain almost 20 percent of the world's fresh surface water. ▼

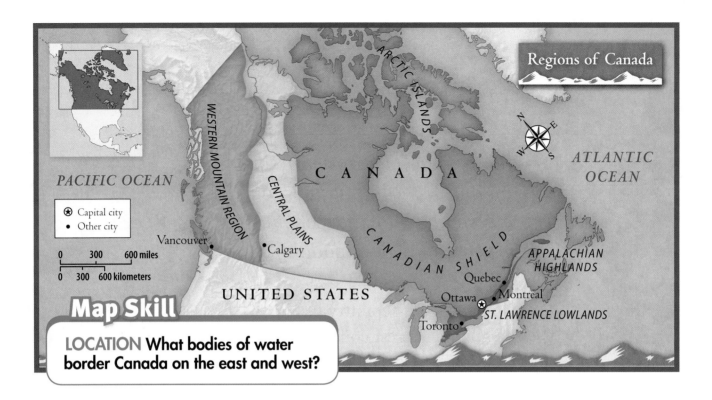

PACIFIC OCEAN

ARCTIC ISLANDS

WESTERN MOUNTAIN REGION

CENTRAL PLAINS

C A N A D A

C A N A D I A N   S H I E L D

ATLANTIC OCEAN

APPALACHIAN HIGHLANDS

⊛ Capital city
• Other city

0   300   600 miles
0   300   600 kilometers

Vancouver

•Calgary

UNITED STATES

Quebec•

Ottawa•⊛ •Montreal
          ST. LAWRENCE LOWLANDS
Toronto•

Map Skill

LOCATION **What bodies of water border Canada on the east and west?**

Ⓑ ST. LAWRENCE LOWLANDS

C A N A D A

ST. LAWRENCE LOWLANDS

APPALACHIAN HIGHLANDS

Canada can be divided into six **regions**. A region is an area with common features. The St. Lawrence Lowlands is the smallest region in Canada. A **lowland** is an area that is lower than the land around it. Most Canadians live here. It is the center of manufacturing, farming, and city life. Many big cities were built here, including Ottawa, the country's capital.

Land and Climate

Locate the St. Lawrence Lowlands on the map above. This region includes the St. Lawrence River and the Canadian Great Lakes. Some of Canada's best farmland is found in this region.

To the east, the Appalachian Highlands are made up of islands with low, rolling hills.

PLACES

Horseshoe Falls is a Canadian waterfall on the Niagara River between Lake Erie and Lake Ontario. It is part of Niagara Falls. Millions of people visit Horseshoe Falls every year. The river that flows into the falls is used to create electricity for cities.

Horseshoe Falls

▲ The St. Lawrence Lowlands have many forests. The trees turn beautiful colors in the fall.

The soil is rich, and the land is flat. Farmers grow many products, including corn, barley, fruit, and vegetables. Other Canadians live and work in this region's large cities, such as Montreal and Toronto.

The St. Lawrence Lowlands have a wonderful climate. It is mild in the spring, hot in the summer, and cold in the winter. There is lots of rain and snow, which keeps the soil rich and the crops healthy.

▲ In the spring, people collect sap from maple trees and make syrup.

Plants and Animals

The forests of the St. Lawrence Lowlands are filled with trees. The leaf of the maple tree is Canada's national symbol.

People collect the sap from maple trees in the spring. They use this sap to make Canada's famous maple syrup. The forests' animals include foxes, squirrels, and rabbits.

Animals such as foxes live in the forests of the St. Lawrence Lowlands. ▼

QUICK CHECK

Main Idea and Details **Why is the soil in the St. Lawrence Lowlands so rich?**

C CANADIAN SHIELD

The Canadian Shield is shaped like a shield carried by an ancient soldier. It also looks like a giant horseshoe. This huge region covers almost half of Canada, yet few people live there.

Land and Climate

The northern part of the Canadian Shield sweeps around the Arctic. The Arctic is bitterly cold, so few people can live there. **Tundra**, a flat area of land without trees, covers this northern land. The ground below the tundra is always frozen.

Thick forests cover most of the remaining land in the Canadian Shield. There are also thousands of lakes and many low hills. To the north, the Arctic Islands are covered in ice. They are one of the world's least populated regions.

Furry animals live in the cold Canadian Shield.

Most trees cannot grow on tundra because it is so cold. In the summer, however, many flowers will bloom.

Plants and Animals

The Canadian Shield tundra is bare most of the year. Just a few types of small plants can grow there. Only in the summer does the land come alive when colorful flowers bloom.

Although trees cannot grow in the northern part of the Canadian Shield, evergreen forests cover the land in the rest of the region. Deer, gray wolves, and moose are some of the forest animals that live there. High above the trees bald eagles sometimes soar though the air, while geese fly above the lakes.

The northern Arctic waters are home to a type of whale called the narwhal. The narwhal has a long, sharp tooth. Another Arctic animal, the polar bear, also lives in Canada's far north.

You can see moose in the Canadian Shield.

QUICK CHECK

Main Idea and Details **Why do so few people live in the Canadian Shield?**

PEOPLE

An Arctic people called the Inuit have lived in the northern part of the Canadian Shield for more than 1,000 years. Although some still build houses from snow, most Inuits now live in wooden homes in towns. Inuit artists create prints and sandstone sculptures. Others work together in local fishing industries.

An Inuit girl

Polar bears are excellent swimmers. The fur on the bottom of their paws keeps them from slipping on the ice.

PLAINS AND MOUNTAINS

WESTERN
MOUNTAIN   CENTRAL
REGION   PLAINS

CANADA

Look back at the map on page 54. Locate the Central Plains and the Western Mountain Region.

Central Plains

The Central Plains of Canada extend from the United States border to the cold Arctic Ocean in the north. **Prairies** stretch across the Central Plains. A prairie is a flat or rolling land covered with grass. Farmers grow grains like wheat and corn in the rich soil. Ranchers graze their cattle on the prairie.

Western Mountain Region

West of the Central Plains are the Canadian Rocky Mountains and the Coast Mountains. The Canadian Rockies begin at the border with the United States and extend north. The weather can change very quickly in the mountains. It is not unusual for the temperature to fall 30 degrees in only a few hours! People love to hike and ski in the Canadian Rockies.

The beaver is a symbol of Canada. It appears on the Canadian nickel.

In the Central Plains of Canada, farmers grow grains, such as wheat.

People can go hiking in the Canadian Rockies.

Plants and Animals

Pine trees grow in the mountain forests, while grass and crops cover the warmer prairies. If you visited the forests of the Central Plains, you would see many animals—moose, elk, deer, and wolves. In the Canadian Rockies, there are also bears, sheep, and mountain goats.

The Canadian beaver lives in parts of the Central Plains. Beavers live near rivers and lakes. With their sharp teeth, these animals cut down tall trees by chewing through the bark. Then they use the fallen trees to make dams in a stream.

QUICK CHECK

Main Idea and Details **What is the land like in the Central Plains?**

Check Understanding

1. **VOCABULARY** Write one sentence for each vocabulary word below.
   lowland   tundra
   region   prairie

2. **READING SKILL Main Idea and Details** Use your chart from page 52 to write a paragraph about Canada's geography.

Main Idea	Details

 3. **Write About It** How does the weather in Canada affect people throughout the year?

Map and Globe Skills
Understand Latitude and Longitude

VOCABULARY

grid

latitude

longitude

degree

Every place on Earth has an address, which tells its exact location. To describe the location of a place, geographers use maps with **grids**. Grids are lines that cross each other on a map. Earth's grid has two sets of lines called **latitude** and **longitude**.

Lines of latitude measure how far north or south a place is from the equator. Lines of longitude measure distance east or west of the prime meridian. Lines of latitude and longitude measure distance on Earth's surface in **degrees**. The symbol for degrees is °.

Learn It

- Look at Map A. Lines of latitude north of the equator are labeled **N**. Lines of latitude south of the equator are labeled **S**.

- Now look at Map B. Lines of longitude east of the prime meridian are labeled **E**. Lines of longitude west of the prime meridian are labeled **W**.

- Lines of latitude and lines of longitude can be used to locate any place on Earth. When you locate places on a map, give the latitude first and longitude second.

Map A

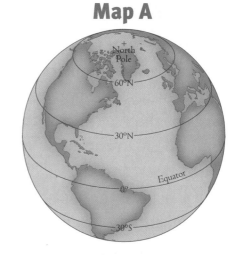

Map B

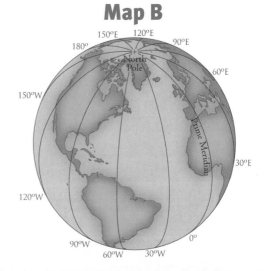

Map C

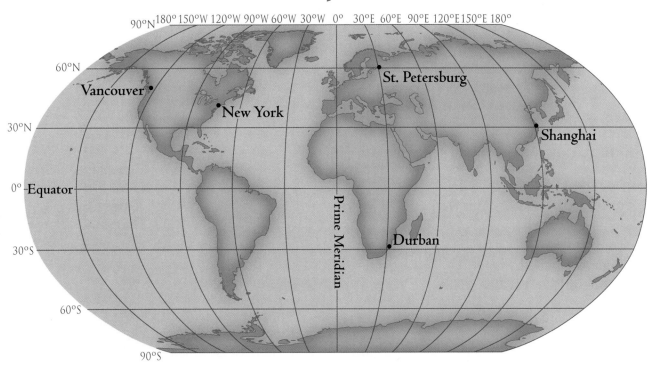

Try It

Use Map C above to answer the questions.

- What line of latitude is at 0 degrees?

- Is Canada east or west of the Prime Meridian?

Apply It

- Give the closest latitude and longitude address of Shanghai.

- Which city is nearest to the address of 30°S, 30°E?

- Find the latitude and longitude closest to Vancouver.

The History of Canada

VOCABULARY

land bridge p. 63

barter p. 64

province p. 66

territory p. 66

confederation p. 66

READING SKILL

Sequence

Copy the sequence chart. As you read, fill it in with important dates in Canada's history.

| First |
| Next |
| Last |

New York Academic Content Standards

2.1, 2.2, 2.3, 2.4, 3.1, 3.2

People moved to Canada's western lands and settled in towns.

VISUAL PREVIEW

How did Canada become a nation?

A Native peoples lived on the land for many years before Europeans arrived.

B Great Britain won a fight with France over control of Canada.

C Today, Canada is a nation of ten provinces and three territories.

Ⓐ EARLY CANADA

When the first Europeans arrived, native Canadians were already living on the land. Canada's name comes from the native Canadian word kanata, which means community.

Many centuries ago, North America and Asia were connected by a strip of land called a **land bridge**. Hunters from Asia came looking for animals to kill and eat.

Early Peoples

These early native Canadians lived in the frozen Arctic. Other native peoples settled in the Canadian Shield and the Atlantic coast. Many years later, European explorers called Vikings reached North America. They founded a colony called Vinland.

European Explorers

Almost 500 years after the Vikings, other European explorers began sailing west. They were looking for a way to get to Asia. Instead, they landed on the east coast of Canada. In 1497 John Cabot claimed the island of Newfoundland for England. Soon large fishing boats from Europe were sailing to Canada.

Native Canadians made artwork like these masks which are worn on top of the head.

QUICK CHECK

Sequence Who were the first Europeans to reach Canada?

EUROPEAN EXPLORERS

French and English explorers arrived in Canada in the 1500s. Over the next 100 years, England and France founded colonies in Canada. In time, these colonies became an independent nation.

The French

In 1535, the French explorer Jacques Cartier sailed up the St. Lawrence River. He reached the area where the cities of Montreal and Quebec are today. Cartier built a fort in Montreal. Another French explorer, Samuel de Champlain, founded the city of Quebec in 1608.

What attracted French explorers to Canada? Canada's natural riches—fish and animal fur. Many people wore fancy hats made from beaver fur. To get fur, the French traded with the Native Canadians. The French traders exchanged goods such as knives and fishhooks. Trading goods without using money is called bartering.

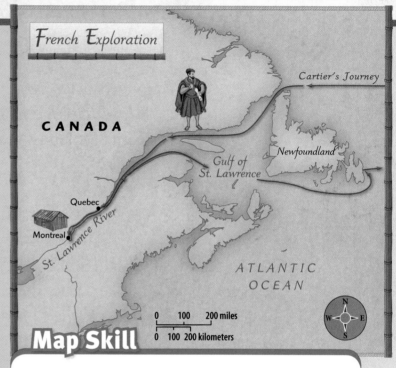

French Exploration

Cartier's Journey

CANADA

Newfoundland

Gulf of St. Lawrence

Quebec

Montreal

St. Lawrence River

ATLANTIC OCEAN

0   100   200 miles
0   100 200 kilometers

Map Skill

LOCATION How far did Cartier travel on the St. Lawrence River?

Jacques Cartier was the first European to explore the St. Lawrence River. ▶

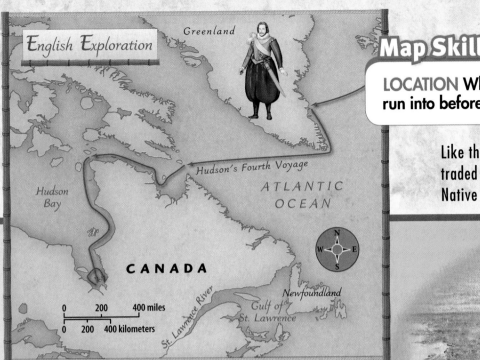

English Exploration

Greenland

Hudson's Fourth Voyage

ATLANTIC OCEAN

Hudson Bay

CANADA

St. Lawrence River

Newfoundland

Gulf of St. Lawrence

0 200 400 miles
0 200 400 kilometers

Map Skill

LOCATION What island did Hudson run into before he reached Canada?

Like the French, the English traded furs with the Native Canadians. ▼

The English

Great Britain also wanted to explore and control Canada's rich land and waters. In 1610 the English explorer Henry Hudson sailed into a body of water. He named it Hudson Bay.

Now both the English and the French were trading with the Native Canadians. Both countries wanted to control trade in Canada. They went to war.

The war has two different names. In Canada, it's called the Seven Years' War. In the United States, it's called the French and Indian War. The war ended in 1763. England, which was now called Great Britain, won control of most of the land.

QUICK CHECK

Sequence When was the city of Quebec founded?

CANADA BECOMES A NATION

Canada is divided into ten provinces and three territories. **Provinces** and **territories** are political areas that make up a country. The difference between a province and a territory is that the national government has more control over a territory than over a province.

Canadian Confederation

On July 1, 1867, the Canadian Confederation was formed. A **confederation** is a group of provinces or territories joined together. The four original provinces of the Canadian Confederation were Quebec, Ontario, Nova Scotia, and New Brunswick. More provinces and territories joined. By 1873 the Confederation stretched all the way from Prince Edward Island to British Columbia and up to the Northwest Territories.

Map Skill

LOCATION **Name the provinces and territories that border the United States.**

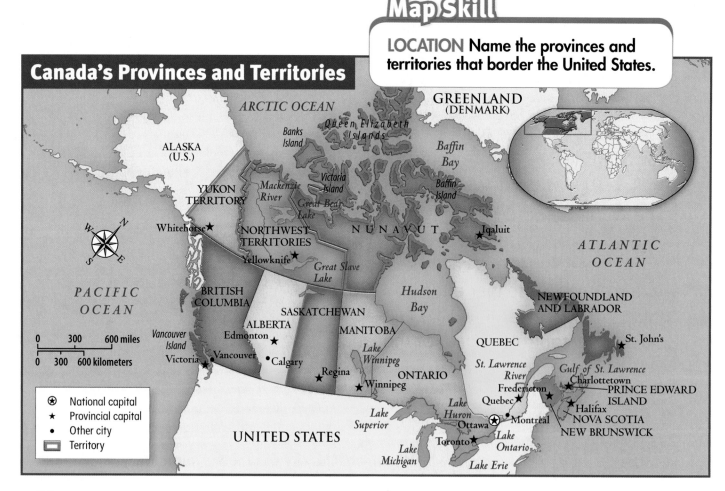

Canada's Provinces and Territories

Legend:
⊛ National capital
★ Provincial capital
• Other city
▭ Territory

EVENT

Nunavut is Canada's newest territory. It used to be part of the Northwest Territories. It was officially formed on April 1, 1999.

Children in Nunavut

Moving West

In 1885, workers finished building a railroad called the Canadian-Pacific Railway. It linked Canada from east to west. More people began to move into the western lands of Canada. In 1905 Alberta and Saskatchewan joined the Confederation.

After Newfoundland joined the Confederation in 1949, it would be fifty years before Canada's map changed again. In 1999 the territory of Nunavut became part of Canada. It's the largest part of Canada, but the fewest people live there. It is very cold!

QUICK CHECK

Sequence **Did Alberta join the Canadian Confederation before or after the Canadian-Pacific Railway was completed?**

Check Understanding

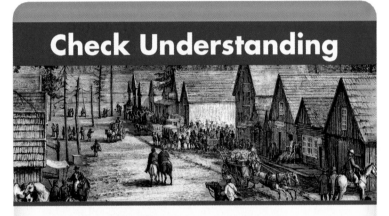

1. **VOCABULARY** Write one sentence for each vocabulary word below.
   barter   **confederation**   **province**

2. **READING SKILL** Sequence Use your chart from page 62 to write a paragraph about the history of Canada.

First
Next
Last

3. **Write About It** How has Canada changed since 1867?

▼ The railroad brought more people to Canada's western provinces and territories.

GOVERNING CANADA

VOCABULARY

federal p. 70

prime minister p. 70

parliament p. 70

READING SKILL

Sequence

Use the chart below to list important events linked to Canada's government.

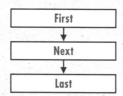

First
Next
Last

New York Academic Content Standards

2.1, 2.2, 2.3, 2.4, 5.1, 5.4

Canada's government is based in Ottawa, the capital city.

VISUAL PREVIEW

How has Canada's government developed over time?

A Canada gained its independence one step at a time.

B Today, Canada has national and local governments.

Ⓐ CANADA AND GREAT BRITAIN

Did you know that the Queen of England is also the Queen of Canada? She does not make the laws, however. Canada has its own government. It is an independent country like the United States.

Great Britain and Canada have a close relationship. As you read in Lesson 2, Great Britain won the Seven Years' War. It was in charge of Canada. But Canadians wanted to make their own decisions and be independent.

▲ The flag of Canada shows the leaf of the maple tree. The flag became official in 1965.

Steps Toward Independence

Canadian independence would not happen all at once. The first step was when the Canadian Confederation was formed in 1867. Then, in 1931, an agreement was made so Canada could make its own laws for the first time. Finally, in 1982, the Queen of England signed a law called the Constitution Act. This important law created a new, independent constitution for Canada.

Citizenship

Charter of Rights and Freedoms

Part of Canada's constitution is the Canadian Charter of Rights and Freedoms. It's like the Bill of Rights in the United States. The Charter names and protects the basic rights of ordinary Canadians.

Write About It Why is the Charter of Rights and Freedoms important?

QUICK CHECK

Sequence When could Canada make its own laws for the first time?

Canada's History

1885 - Canadian-Pacific Railway is finished.

1913 - More than 400,000 new people immigrate to Canada.

1850

1900

1867 - Four provinces unite to form Canada.

1896 - Gold is found along the Yukon River.

B GOVERNING CANADA

Primary Sources

In 1993 Kim Campbell became the first woman prime minister of Canada. To improved eduction, she said: "I have instructed all federal government departments to donate their old computer systems . . . to Canada's schools. . . . Our goal is to have every school in Canada electronically connected."

[From a speech given August 16, 1993]

✎ **Write About It** Write a letter to Canada's Prime Minister with an idea about how to improve your school.

Like the United States, Canada has a **federal** government. In a federal government, the power of government is shared between national and local levels.

Three Branches

The **prime minister** runs Canada's government. He or she leads the executive branch, which carries out the laws. Canada does not have a Congress like the United States. Instead, it has a **parliament**. A parliament is the legislative branch of government. Parliament makes the country's laws.

Canada's judicial branch is made up of many courts. The Supreme Court of Canada is the highest court in the country. It decides whether or not laws are fair. It also can say whether a law is allowed under Canada's constitution.

1949 - Newfoundland becomes the last province to join Canada.

1965 - The flag of Canada is approved.

1999 - Nunavut is formed.

1950

2000

1931 - Canada can make its own laws for the first time in its history.

1982 - Canada writes its own constitution.

▲ Queen Elizabeth signed the Constitution Act on April 17, 1982.

Local Governments

Each province and territory in Canada has its own government, too. Canada's local governments pass laws that affect the daily lives of the citizens. This includes building new roads or improving schools.

QUICK CHECK

Sequence **When did Newfoundland join Canada?**

The Supreme Court Building is in Ottawa. ▼

Check Understanding

1. **VOCABULARY** Write a short paragraph about Canada's government. Use each vocabulary word below

   federal   **prime minister**   **parliament**

2. **READING SKILL Sequence**
   Use your sequence chart from page 68 to write a paragraph about the government of Canada.

First
Next
Last

3. **Write About It** How did Canada become independent?

Canada at Work

VOCABULARY

manufacturing p. 73

industry p. 73

product p. 73

international trade p. 76

READING SKILL

Sequence
Use the chart below to fill in the steps that a raw material must go through to become a product that is exported.

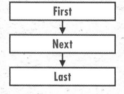

First
↓
Next
↓
Last

New York Academic Content Standards
3.1, 3.2, 4.1, 4.2

These logs will be turned into furniture and paper and then sent all over the world.

VISUAL PREVIEW

How does Canada's economy grow and change?

A Manufacturing and service industries are growing in Canada.

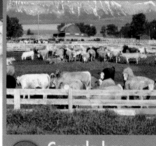

B Canada has turned its natural resources into big businesses.

C Canada's economy has gone global by trading with other countries.

Ⓐ A CHANGING ECONOMY

If you had visited Canada 200 years ago, you would have met farmers, fishermen, hunters, and loggers. Today, many Canadians work in different kinds of jobs.

Canada's economy is changing. Many years ago, most Canadians worked on the land. They farmed, fished, or cut down trees. Today, many Canadians have **manufacturing** jobs. Manufacturing means making goods using machines. The manufacturing of cars, trucks, airplanes, and their parts is the largest industry in Canada. An **industry** is a business that makes one kind of product. A **product** is anything that is made or created.

▲ Airplane parts are manufactured in Canada.

Wood Products

The wood products industry is very important in Canada. As you have learned, Canada has many forests. Trees are cut down, and the logs are cut into boards. The boards, called lumber, are then used to make furniture. Logs are also ground into a pulp and made into paper.

Services

Almost three-quarters of Canada's citizens work in service industries. Service industries include jobs where workers help someone else. Workers in education, health care, banks, and stores are all service industry workers.

Park rangers are service industry workers. ▼

QUICK CHECK

Sequence How has Canada's economy changed over the years?

NATURAL RESOURCES

Canada is rich in natural resources. As you learned in Unit 1, natural resources are materials found in nature that people use. Most things you use every day start as raw, natural resources. The food you eat is first grown on a farm or caught in the ocean. The paper you write on begins as wood cut down in a forest.

Forests

Canada's forests are important for logging. Loggers cut down many kinds of trees, including pine and cedar. Then other Canadian workers turn these logs into wood products, such as paper and lumber.

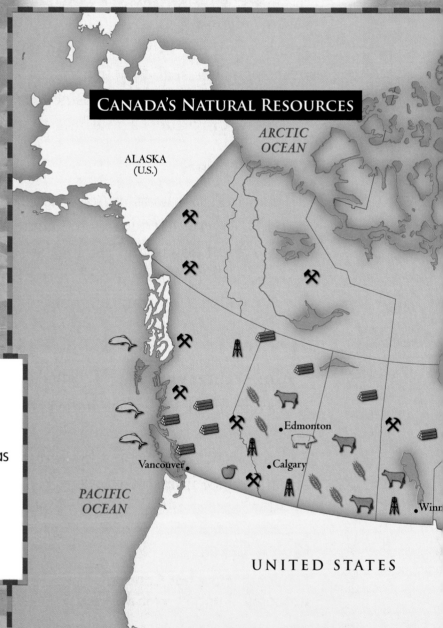

CANADA'S NATURAL RESOURCES

ARCTIC OCEAN

ALASKA (U.S.)

Edmonton

Vancouver

Calgary

PACIFIC OCEAN

Winn

UNITED STATES

Legend			
✪	National capital	🍎	Fruit
•	Other city	🦞	Lobster
—	National boundary	⚒	Mining
—	Other boundary	⛽	Natural Gas
🐂	Cattle	🐓	Poultry
🐄	Dairy	🐖	Pork
🐟	Fish	🦪	Scallops
🪵	Forest Products	🌾	Wheat

Farming

Most of Canada's rich farmland is in the prairie. Canada's most important farm products are wheat, milk, vegetables, fruit, cattle, pork, and chicken.

Mining

Canada is also rich in minerals, which are natural resources that are not plants or animals. These minerals include metals, such as copper, gold, silver, and iron.

GREENLAND

Baffin Bay

Hudson Bay

ATLANTIC OCEAN

Montreal

★ Ottawa

Toronto

| 0 | 300 | 600 miles |

| 0 | 300 | 600 kilometers |

Fishing

Fishing is also an important industry. People fish near Newfoundland and along the Pacific coast.

QUICK CHECK

Sequence **Where does paper come from?**

International trade, which is trade between different countries, is very important to Canada's economy.

Canada Buys and Sells

Canada's most important trading partner is the United States. That means that most goods exported from Canada are sold in our country. Also, most goods imported to, or brought into, Canada are made in the United States.

Canada imports computers, fruits, vegetables, chemicals, and different kinds of machinery from around the world. Canada also buys lots of cars and trucks made in other countries.

Since Canadian farmers grow more wheat than the country needs, they export the extra wheat to other countries. Canada also sells cars, trucks, and automobile parts made in Canadian factories. Wood products like furniture and paper are also valuable exports.

Canadian products are placed in containers and exported to other countries. ▼

▲ Plants along the Niagara River create electricity. Canada exports extra electricity to the United States.

Transportation and Trade

In the 1600s, boats and canoes carried people and goods across Canada's lakes and rivers. Then, in 1885 the Canadian Pacific Railway connected Canada from coast to coast.

Today Canadians use different kinds of transportation. Railroads connect cities and towns. The Trans-Canada highway carries goods across the country, from the east to the west coast. Other highways extend south and connect cities in Canada and the United States.

QUICK CHECK

Sequence **Why do Canadian farmers export wheat to other countries?**

Check Understanding

1. **VOCABULARY** Write one sentence for each vocabulary word below.
   manufacturing   product
   industry   import

2. **READING SKILL Sequence** Use your chart from page 72 to write a paragraph about how a raw material becomes an export item.

   | First |
   | Next |
   | Last |

3. **Write About It** How has the economy of Canada changed over time?

Chart and Graph Skills

Use Bar Graphs

VOCABULARY

graph

bar graph

You have read about how changes in Canada's population helped the country grow. You can see some information about these population changes by reading a **graph**. A graph is a special kind of picture that shows information in a way that is easy to understand. A **bar graph** uses bars to show information. You can use bar graphs to compare different amounts.

Learn It

Look at the graph below as you follow the steps.

- **Read the title.** The graph shows the population of Canada between 1901 and 2001.

- **Read the labels.** The labels along the bottom show the years the graph is about. The column at the far left shows the number of people in millions.

- **Put the information together.** Put your finger at the top of the purple bar. Then move your finger to the left. You can see that the purple bar reaches the mark for thirty million. That means thirty million people lived in Canada in 2001. In which year did Canada have its lowest population?

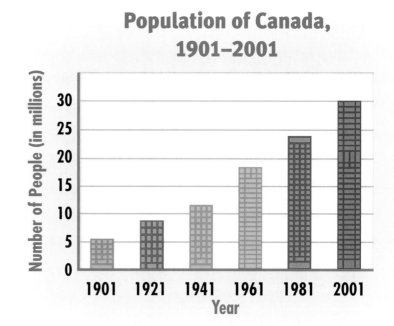

Population of Canada, 1901–2001

Try It

▲ Quebec

Now look at the graph to the right to answer the questions.

- What does the graph show?

- What do the bars stand for?

- When did the most people live in Quebec?

Apply It

Count the number of students in your class on each day of one week during the school year. Then make a bar graph to show the information. Decide which information will go along the bottom and side of the graph. Give your graph a title.

Population of Quebec, 1901–2001

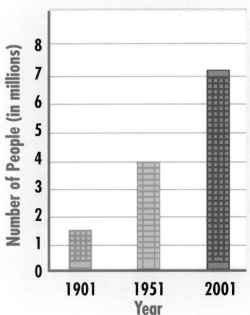

Lesson 5

VOCABULARY

bilingual p. 82

ancestor p. 82

tourist p. 84

READING SKILL

Main Idea and Details
Use the chart below to fill in details about life in Canada.

Main Idea	Details

New York Academic Content Standards
2.1, 2.2, 2.3, 2.4, 3.1

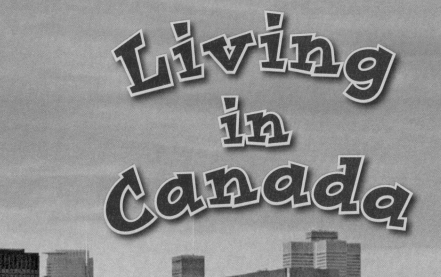

Living in Canada

Montreal is a modern city of great beauty.

VISUAL PREVIEW

How has life in Canada changed?

A Large cities and small towns and communities have developed in Canada.

B Montreal has blended its French and English history.

C Canadian culture attracts people from around the world.

Ⓐ CITIES AND TOWNS

Montreal gets its name from a nearby mountain, Mount Royal. Toronto's name comes from a native word meaning "where there are trees standing in the water."

Montreal is one of the most important cities in Canada. Like Mexico City, it is a major center of culture, education, and business. Montreal has the second-largest population in the country.

Toronto has the largest population. People from all over the world come into Toronto every day to do business. The city is home to theaters, museums, and the Hockey Hall of Fame.

▲ Banff is located at the foot of the Canadian Rockies.

Smaller Communities

There are also smaller communities in Canada. The town of Banff is part of a national park near the Canadian Rockies. It was founded in 1884 as a result of the Canadian Pacific Railway.

Vancouver is a major city located on Canada's west coast. ▼

QUICK CHECK

Main Idea and Details **When did the town of Banff form?**

▲ The Place des Arts is home to many of Montreal's theaters and museums.

▲ The oldest part of Montreal is called the Old City. The streets are paved with small stones.

ⓑ MONTREAL

In Lesson 2, you learned that the French explorer Jacques Cartier settled the area of present-day Montreal. French culture can still be seen and heard there today. In fact, many people in the city speak French and English. Someone who speaks two languages is **bilingual**. More than half of Montreal's citizens have French **ancestors**. Ancestors are a person's relatives from long ago.

Being a Student in Montreal

There are two kinds of schools in Montreal. In some schools, students are taught only in French. In other schools, they speak English. Many Montreal students enjoy reading *Anne of Green Gables* by the famous Canadian author Lucy Maud Montgomery.

▲ Road signs in Montreal are in French and English.

QUICK CHECK

Main Idea and Details **What two languages might you hear in a restaurant in Montreal?**

The Population of Five Canadian Cities

Canada has many large cities. The bar graph below shows the population of five large Canadian cities. Look at the bar graph and the map below. Then answer the questions.

Population: Five Large Cities

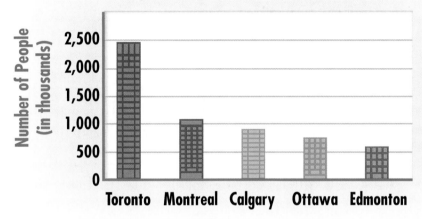

Canada: Five Major Cities

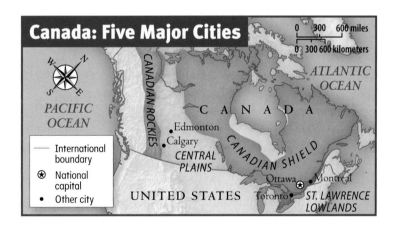

Think About the Population of Canada's Cities

1. Which Canadian city has the largest population?

2. What is the name of the region where three of Canada's largest cities are located?

The Royal Winnipeg Ballet is the oldest ballet company in Canada. ▶

© CANADIAN CULTURE

There is much to see and do in Canada. Canada has a rich cultural life. Citizens and visitors go to plays, musical events, and museums. There are many things to do outdoors too. Each year millions of **tourists** visit Canadian cities. Tourists are people who travel to different places for enjoyment.

Dance and Art

Do you like to dance? Then you might love going to a ballet performance in Winnipeg. Do you like to draw? Then visit the Museum of Fine Arts in Montreal. This is one of the oldest museums in Canada. Children and their parents enjoy seeing the museum's many paintings. This museum also includes a collection of Inuit art.

▲ The Calgary Stampede is a big rodeo that takes place every year in the city of Calgary. Rodeo is a sport where people ride bulls and horses.

Sculpting, or carving, big blocks of ice is a popular winter activity. ▶

Outdoor Activities

Canadian children play outside in their communities, in parks, and in school. During the winter, children enjoy ice skating, skiing, and ice hockey—the most popular sport in Canada.

In Calgary, you can ski and snowboard in Canada Olympic Park. This park was part of the 1988 Winter Olympic Games. In 2010 the Winter Olympics will come to Canada again—this time to Vancouver!

QUICK CHECK

Main Idea and Details What are some examples of activities that tourists enjoy doing in Canada?

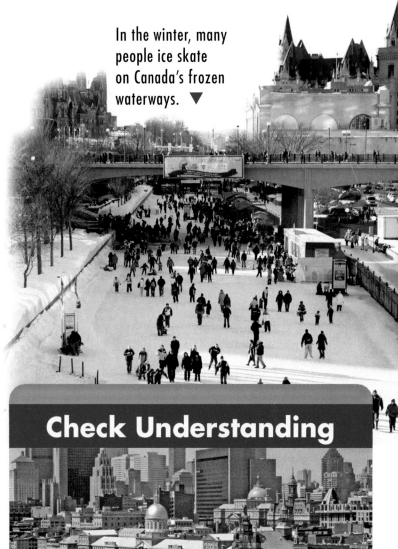

In the winter, many people ice skate on Canada's frozen waterways. ▼

Check Understanding

1. **VOCABULARY** Write a postcard to a friend about a visit to Montreal. Use each vocabulary word below.
   bilingual   **ancestor**
   tourist

2. **READING SKILL** Main Idea and Details Use your chart from page 80 to write a paragraph about life in Canada.

Main Idea	Details

3. **Write About It** How has Montreal changed over time?

Unit 2 Review and Assess

Vocabulary

Number a paper from 1 to 4. Beside each number write the word from the list below that matches the number.

coastline   **province**

industry   **prime minister**

1. a business that makes one kind of product

2. the national leader who runs the Canadian government

3. a political area that makes up a country

4. land along the ocean

Comprehension and Critical Thinking

5. How did the earliest peoples reach Canada?

6. What is tundra?

7. Reading Skills How many provinces did Canada have before 1949?

8. Critical Thinking How is Canada's government similar to the governments of both the United States and Great Britain?

Skill

Use Bar Graphs

Write a complete sentence to answer each question.

9. Which industry employs the most workers in Canada?

10. Which industry employs the smallest number of workers?

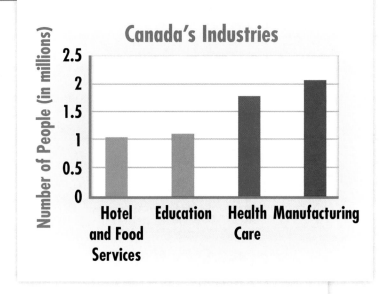

Canada's Industries

New York English Language Arts Test Preparation

*D*irections

Read this passage about the fur trade in Quebec. Then answer questions 1 through 3.

In 1608 Quebec was founded by the French as a fur trading post. But the English wanted to control the fur trade. The English came to Canada. They exchanged European goods with the native Canadians. In return they received valuable beaver furs. These furs were made into expensive hats that were sold in Europe. In 1763, Great Britain won control of most French land in Canada. Now the English controlled most of the fur trade. They began exploring the western lands looking for more beaver and other animals.

---

1 Why was Quebec founded?

  A It gave the French a place to live.

  B It was set up as a fur-trading post.

  C The French wanted to control the western lands of Canada.

  D The English were interested in beaver furs.

2 Which of the following best describes the main idea of this passage?

  A The French settled Canada.

  B The fur trade led to the settlement of Canada by both the French and English.

  C Quebec is a French city.

  D Great Britain turned fur into hats.

3 What was a result of the British winning control of most French land?

  A More French came to Canada.

  B Beaver fur was made into hats.

  C The English gained control of most of the Canadian fur trade.

  D Quebec was founded.

How does a country change over time?

Write About the Big Idea

Expository Paragraph

Think about the different events in Canadian history that you read about in Unit 2. Complete the Foldable with some of these important events and dates. Once you have completed the Foldable, use it to help you write a short paragraph that answers the Big Idea question, "How does a country change over time?" Be sure to list the correct sequence of events in your paragraph. End with a conclusion that summarizes what you've learned about Canadian history.

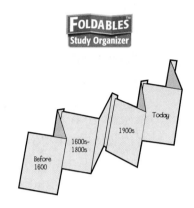

FOLDABLES™
Study Organizer

Before 1600 · 1600s–1800s · 1900s · Today

Make a Book About Canada

Work in small groups to make a book about Canada. Your book should include information about two important places, people, and events in Canada's history.

1. Brainstorm a list of important people, places, and events in Canada's history. Choose two of each from the list.

2. Have two students work together to find a few important facts about each person, place, and event.

3. Each person can then add the information about one person, place, or event to a page for your book.

When your group has finished writing the six pages, join all of the pages together to make a class book about Canada. Display the book in your classroom.

Unit 3

EXPLORE The Big Idea

Essential Question
How do people change the place where they live?

FOLDABLES Study Organizer

Summarize
Make a vertical Trifold Book Foldable to take notes as you read Unit 3. Label the columns **Land Formations**, **Apartheid**, and **Natural Resources**.

Land Formations	Apartheid	Natural Resources

LOG ON
For more about Unit 3, go to
www.macmillanmh.com

SOUTH AFRICA
The Rainbow Nation

PEOPLE, PLACES, AND EVENTS

Dr. Christiaan Barnard

Cape Town

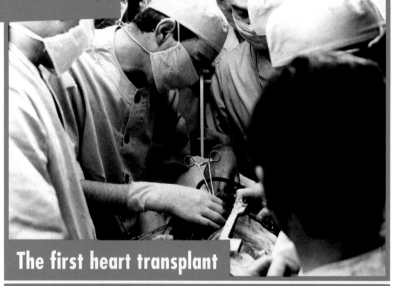

The first heart transplant

1967
The first heart transplant was done at Groote Schuur Hospital in Cape Town, South Africa.

Christiaan Barnard was a South African doctor. In 1967 he did the **first heart transplant**. It was performed in **Cape Town**. **Today** doctors around the world use many of the methods that Dr. Barnard invented.

LOG ON

For more about People, Places, and Events visit
www.macmillanmh.com

Nelson Mandela

Robben Island Prison

South Africa's first open election

1994

Millions of South Africans stood in line to vote in 1994. Nelson Mandela became the country's first black president.

Nelson Mandela was put in **Robben Island Prison** for fighting for fair treatment of blacks in South Africa. After he was free, he was **elected South Africa's first black president**. Today he works for education and world peace.

Lesson 1

VOCABULARY

veld p. 93

game reserve p. 96

safari p. 96

READING SKILL

Summarize

Use the chart below to summarize what you learn about South Africa's geography.

```
┌──────┐  ┌──────┐  ┌──────┐
│      │  │      │  │      │
└──┬───┘  └──┬───┘  └──┬───┘
   │         │         │
   ▼         ▼         ▼
┌──────────────────────────┐
│        Summary           │
└──────────────────────────┘
```

New York Academic Content Standards

3.1, 3.2, 4.1

The Land of South Africa

Most of South Africa's land is high land.

VISUAL PREVIEW

How do people adjust to South Africa's geography?

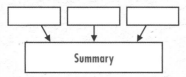

A South Africa's land varies, but most people live in the low lands.

B People live differently near the mountains, rivers, and deserts.

C People have created parks and preserves to protect the wildlife.

D South Africans mine both diamonds and gold.

SOUTH AFRICA'S GEOGRAPHY

Do you like climbing snowy mountains?
How about sitting on sunny beaches?
South Africa has both kinds of places—and more!

South Africa has all kinds of geography. It has rain forests. It has deserts. It has deep valleys and high mountains. It has beautiful beaches.

High and Low Lands

Two-thirds of South Africa is high land. But only a small percentage of the people live on it. It is too dry and hot! The east has many mountains. They rise high above the land. The beaches are the lowest points in South Africa. There are many beaches along the coast.

South Africa also has wide, flat areas usually covered in grass and low bushes. These are called **velds**. The center of the country is a high, dry plateau. South Africa also has low, flat plains and even a large desert in the northwestern part of the country.

QUICK CHECK

Summarize Why do so few people live in South Africa's high land?

Map Skill

LOCATION What two oceans border South Africa?

B MANY DIFFERENT LANDFORMS

There are many amazing sights in South Africa. The places pictured on this page are important parts of South Africa's geography.

1 The Kalahari Desert is a large desert that spreads over three countries in Africa. Part of the Kalahari Desert can be found in South Africa's northwest.

2 The coast in the town of Noordhoek is very long and wide. Noordhoek is part of Cape Town, one of South Africa's three capital cities.

3 There are many vineyards in an area called Western Cape. The soil and climate there are good for growing grapes. It can rain a lot, too. If it rains too much, it can harm the grapevines and ruin the crops.

5

The Drakensberg Mountains are the highest mountains in South Africa. One peak is 11,400 feet high! The name means "dragon mountains."

KALAHARI DESERT

1

Pretoria

Johannesburg

5

NORTHERN CAPE

Bloemfontein

Orange River

3

4

N
W   E
S

DRAKENSBERG

EASTERN CAPE

WESTERN CAPE

Cape Town

2

Port Elizabeth

0   100   200 miles
0   100   200 kilometers

4

The Orange River is South Africa's longest river. It is about 1,300 miles long! It flows west and empties into the Atlantic Ocean.

QUICK CHECK

Summarize **What are three geographical features in South Africa?**

Kruger National Park is the largest game reserve in South Africa.

C NATURAL WONDERS

Some people say that South Africa has the greatest wildlife show on earth. Can you guess why? It is because South Africa has so many different animals!

Animals and Plants

South Africa's creatures range from A to Z—antelopes to zebras—with many other animals in between. Most of these animals live on **game reserves**, land set aside for animals. Animals are protected from hunters in game reserves.

Many people go on **safaris**. A safari is a trip to an African game reserve. You can hear the thunder of elephants marching. In the grass, you might see cheetahs and lions.

▲ People call the baobab tree the "upside-down tree." Does it look like it is growing upside down to you?

The King Protea flower is the national flower of South Africa. It can grow to over six and a half feet tall! ▶

There are more than 20,000 plant species in South Africa. The baobab tree, the King Protea, and pincushion flower are just a few interesting plants. Some plants, like daisies, can be found in the United States as well as South Africa.

QUICK CHECK

Summarize **What happens to animals that live on game reserves?**

You may think that penguins live only at the South Pole. They also live on South Africa's west coast. That is because the cold Antarctic current flows by. ▲

DataGraphic
South Africa's Animals

Which country has the world's fastest animal and the world's tallest bird? You guessed it—South Africa! Kruger National Park is home to many of these animals.

Animal Facts

Tallest Animal	Giraffe	18 feet tall
Fastest Animal	Cheetah	70 miles per hour
Largest Land Animal	African Bush Elephant	15,000 pounds
Largest Reptile	Leatherback Turtle	1,800 pounds
Tallest Bird	Ostrich	9 feet tall

Number of Animals in Kruger National Park

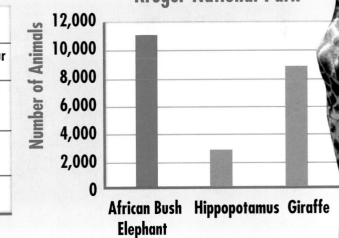

Think About South Africa's Animals

1. How heavy is the world's largest land animal?

2. Find the name of the world's tallest animal. How many of these live in Kruger National Park?

▼ This is what diamonds look like before they are processed.

▼ Diamonds are then polished and inspected by professionals.

▼ A diamond can now be made into jewelry.

South Africa has some of the largest and most important mineral resources in the world. A mineral is a resource found in nature that is not an animal or plant. Diamonds, gold, copper, and silver are all types of minerals.

Diamonds

In 1867 a young boy named Erasmus Jacobs found a large, strange-looking rock by the Orange River. He showed it to his parents. They shouted, "It's a diamond!" When people heard about his discovery, they raced to that area to mine diamonds. Many diamonds have been found in South Africa since then.

▼ Miners found many of the world's largest diamonds at the Big Hole in Kimberley, South Africa. It is the largest hole in the world dug by people, not machines.

◀ It can be quite dark in the gold mines! Mined gold is sometimes molded into bricks.

Gold

South Africa supplies the world with hundreds of tons of gold each year. For hundreds of years, people heard rumors of gold in South Africa. Many people came from all over the world to find it and get rich. They did not find much until one day in 1886.

That day, someone stumbled across a rock in Witwatersrand, a low mountain range. When he looked down, he saw gold! The small chunk of gold was part of miles of gold fields. Today, people come from all over Africa to work in these goldfields.

QUICK CHECK

Summarize **What minerals are found in South Africa?**

Check Understanding

1. **VOCABULARY** Use these words to write a postcard about a visit to South Africa.

   game reserve   safari

2. **READING SKILL** Summarize Use your chart from page 92 to write a paragraph about South Africa's geography.

3. **Write About It** Write a paragraph about how people have changed South Africa's geography.

Map and Globe Skills
Use Intermediate Directions

VOCABULARY

cardinal direction

intermediate direction

You know that the compass rose on a map shows north, east, south, and west. These are **cardinal directions**. A compass rose can also show **intermediate directions**. An intermediate direction is halfway between two cardinal directions.

Learn It

Follow these steps for using a compass rose to find the cardinal and intermediate directions.

- The long points of the compass rose show the cardinal directions. The letters **N**, **E**, **S**, and **W** stand for north, east, south, and west.

- The short points of the compass rose show the intermediate directions. For example, northeast is halfway between north and east. The abbreviations NE, SE, SW, and NW stand for northeast, southeast, southwest, and northwest. Intermediate directions are not always labeled on a compass rose.

Pretoria is one of South Africa's three capital cities. ▼

Try It

Look at the map below. It shows South Africa's nine provinces. They are like states.

- In which direction would a person from Northern Cape go to visit a person from Gauteng?

- If you lived in KwaZulu-Natal, in what direction would you travel to reach Eastern Cape?

- Is Mpumalanga northeast or southeast of Western Cape?

Apply It

- Find Kroonstad on the map. Is it northeast or northwest of Durban?

- Find Pretoria. Is it southeast or northeast of Cape Town?

- Find Kimberley. Is it east or southwest of Johannesburg?

- Which city is southwest of Bloemfontein: Cape Town or Pretoria?

South Africa

National capital
Other city

ZIMBABWE
MOZAMBIQUE
BOTSWANA
LIMPOPO
GAUTENG
NAMIBIA
NORTH-WEST
Pretoria
MPUMALANGA
Johannesburg
Kroonstad
SWAZILAND
Kimberley
FREE STATE
Bloemfontein
KWAZULU-NATAL
Durban
NORTHERN CAPE
LESOTHO
EASTERN CAPE
INDIAN OCEAN
Cape Town
WESTERN CAPE
East London
Port Elizabeth
ATLANTIC OCEAN
0   100   200 miles
0   100 200 kilometers

Lesson 2

VOCABULARY
Boer p. 104

apartheid p. 105

homeland p. 105

READING SKILL
Summarize
Use the chart below to summarize what you learn about South Africa's history.

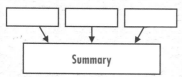

Summary

New York Academic Content Standards
2.1, 2.2, 2.3, 2.4, 5.1

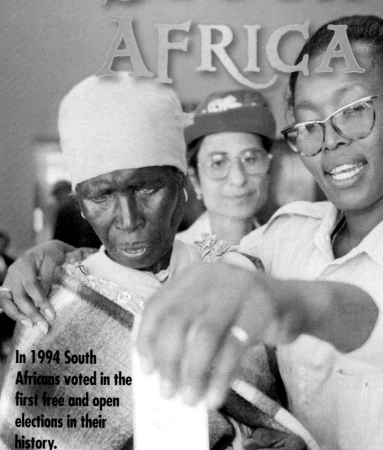

THE HISTORY OF SOUTH AFRICA

In 1994 South Africans voted in the first free and open elections in their history.

How has South Africa changed throughout its history?

A The first people in South Africa hunted animals and gathered plants.

B Europeans came to South Africa and fought over control of the country.

C Blacks began fighting a law that separated blacks and whites.

D Today, all South Africans can vote and have hope for the future.

A THE FIRST SOUTH AFRICANS

Who were the first people in South Africa?
How were they able to live?

South Africa is home to perhaps our oldest human ancestors in the world. Scientists have found proof of our early humans in South Africa that date back over 50,000 years!

San and Khoikhoi

We do not know much about those early ancestors. We do know that other people came to South Africa about 20,000 years ago. First came the San people. They constantly traveled, hunting animals and gathering food to eat. Later, the Khoikhoi people lived in South Africa. Like the San, the Khoikhoi lived off the land. However, the Khoikhoi also farmed and raised animals, such as sheep and cattle.

QUICK CHECK

Summarize Who were the first groups to settle in South Africa?

▼ The rock paintings of the San are thousands of years old.

Many groups knew that South Africa was a good place to live. In 1652 the Dutch decided to settle in South Africa. This would allow them to get food to their sailors traveling from Holland to India.

Fighting Over South Africa

The Dutch settlers were known as the **Boers**, a dutch word that means "farmer." Over time, French and German people joined the Dutch. Yet, not everyone got along. In 1795 the British took over the community. The Boers did not want the British telling them what to do. The Zulu, who also lived there, did not want to lose their land.

The Boers, British, and Zulu fought many battles in the 1800s. Eventually, the British gained control of South Africa.

▲ This Zulu boy is wearing a native costume.

QUICK CHECK

Summarize **Who fought for control of South Africa in the 1800s?**

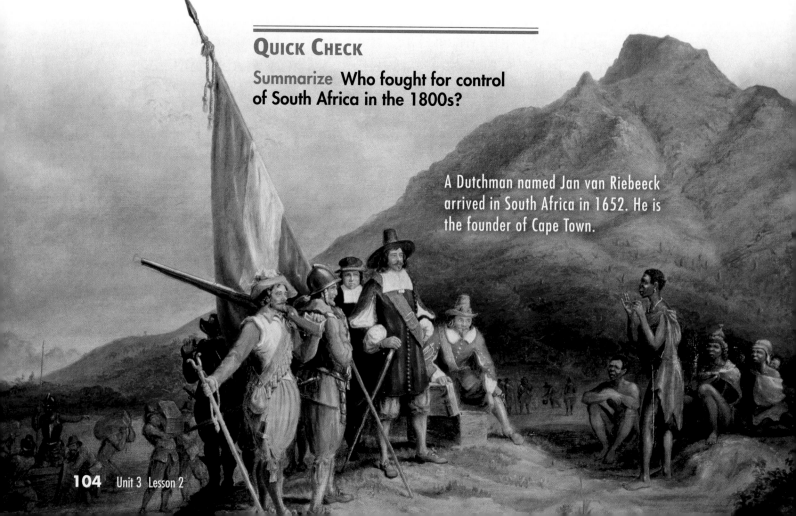

A Dutchman named Jan van Riebeeck arrived in South Africa in 1652. He is the founder of Cape Town.

▲ Apartheid separated blacks from whites. Many fought to end apartheid.

Ⓒ A DIVIDED SOUTH AFRICA

White people continued to rule South Africa. They did not treat the black people fairly. In 1948 the government started the policy of **apartheid**. Look at the word. Do you see "apart" in it? Apartheid means that black people and white people had to live apart.

Apartheid

The government divided South Africa into white and black areas. The whites got most of the land. The blacks had to live in the poorest parts, called **homelands**. The land in the homelands was not good for farming.

Black people in South Africa fought hard to have equal rights. Nelson Mandela helped lead the fight to end apartheid. Apartheid finally fell apart, piece by piece, in the early 1990s.

PEOPLE

When Frederik Willem de Klerk was president of South Africa, he agreed to end apartheid. He released Nelson Mandela from prison. In 1993 Mandela and de Klerk won the Nobel Peace Prize for ending apartheid.

F.W. de Klerk

QUICK CHECK

Summarize What was apartheid?

It was April 1994. People stood in line for hours, even days. The lines stretched for miles. The hot sun beat down, but no one complained. People smiled and laughed! What could make them so happy?

The First Open Election

For the first time in South Africa's history, every person over the age of 18 could vote. It did not matter if you were black or white. A new government was created on that day. It would be led by a new president.

Nelson Mandela was elected as the first black president of South Africa. He said:

"The time for healing wounds has come. . . . The time to build is upon us.**"**

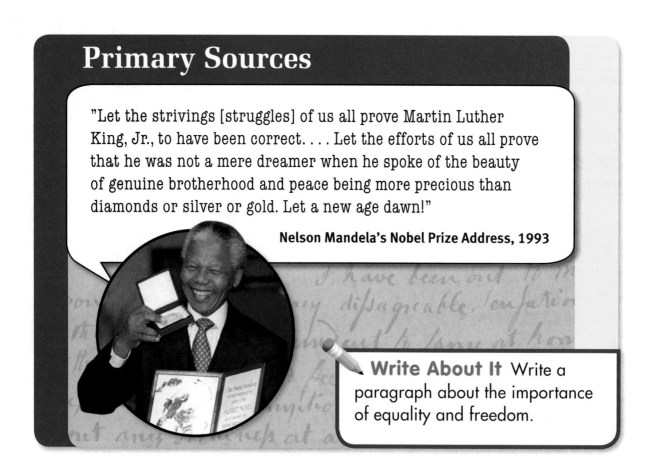

Primary Sources

"Let the strivings [struggles] of us all prove Martin Luther King, Jr., to have been correct. . . . Let the efforts of us all prove that he was not a mere dreamer when he spoke of the beauty of genuine brotherhood and peace being more precious than diamonds or silver or gold. Let a new age dawn!"

Nelson Mandela's Nobel Prize Address, 1993

Write About It Write a paragraph about the importance of equality and freedom.

Hundreds of South Africans waited in line to vote in April, 1994.

EVENT

Each year on April 27, South Africans celebrate Freedom Day. On this day in 1994, South Africa had its first democratic election. They elected Nelson Mandela president.

Freedom Day

Hope for the Future

South Africa faced great changes, but the land was filled with hope. Many black children went to school for the first time. South African businesses started to hire black workers instead of just white workers. The new government gives support to businesses that hire black workers. During apartheid, many companies from other countries refused to come to South Africa. Now they are building factories and creating new jobs.

QUICK CHECK

Summarize **How did people feel about the end of apartheid?**

Check Understanding

1. **VOCABULARY** Use the words below to write a paragraph about South Africa.
   apartheid   homeland

2. **READING SKILL Summarize**
   Use your chart from page 102 to write a paragraph about South Africa's history.

 3. **Write About It** Write a paragraph about how apartheid changed life for black South Africans.

VOCABULARY

environment p. 109

checks and balances p. 111

READING SKILL

Summarize
Use the chart below to summarize what you learn about South Africa's government.

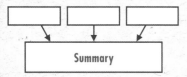

Summary

New York Academic Content Standards
2.1, 2.3, 2.4, 5.1, 5.3

Governing South Africa

South Africa's president gives a speech to lawmakers in Cape Town. Cape Town is one of South Africa's three capital cities.

VISUAL PREVIEW

How has South Africa's government changed?

A South Africa's new constitution promises basic rights, such as education.

B South Africa's government now has three branches that share power.

A A NEW PLAN

As you read in Lesson 2, the year 1994 was the first time everyone in South Africa could vote. At last everyone had equal power to make change in their government.

The new government started by writing a new constitution, a written plan of government. The lawmakers had a great idea. First, they read the laws of other governments. Then, they took the best parts. They added many ideas of their own, too.

Bill of Rights

An important part of the South African constitution is the Bill of Rights. It is similar to the U.S. Bill of Rights. The South African Bill of Rights offers its citizens many rights—health care, education, freedom, and a healthy **environment**. The environment is the air, water, land, and all living things around us.

▲ Nelson Mandela signed the new constitution into law in 1996.

QUICK CHECK

Summarize **What rights does the South African Bill of Rights promise?**

The South African Bill of Rights says that everyone has the right to an education. ▶

THREE BRANCHES OF GOVERNMENT

Like the U.S. government, the South African government has a legislative branch, an executive branch, and a judicial branch.

How the Government is Set Up

The legislative branch is called Parliament. Parliament makes laws. It is made up the National Council of Provinces and the National Assembly. Each province of South Africa has an equal number of members in the National Council of Provinces.

Members of the National Assembly are elected by the people of South Africa. The National Assembly elects someone to be the president of South Africa. The president is the head of the executive branch.

The judicial branch is made up of many courts that decide whether or not someone has broken a law. The top court is called the Supreme Court of Appeal. There is an even higher court that decides if laws are constitutional. This is called the Constitutional Court.

Leaders of South Africa's native peoples play a role in the government. President Thabo Mbeki (left) shakes hands with a Zulu chief. ▼

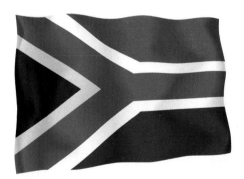

▲ The "Y" in the flag stands for South Africa's different groups coming together into one nation.

Citizenship

Checks and Balances

South Africa's government has a system of **checks and balances**. Each branch of government can check, or stop, the work of the other. This balances their actions and makes them fair. For example, the president is elected by the members of Parliament. The president has the power, however, to stop Parliament from passing a new law. In this way, the president can check the power of Parliament.

Write About It Why is it important to have checks and balances?

Three Capitals

The United States has only one capital—Washington, D.C. South Africa has three capitals!

Each capital is the home of a branch of the government. Pretoria is the executive capital. The president's offices are in Pretoria. Cape Town is the legislative capital. The buildings of Parliament are located there. Bloemfontein is the judicial capital. The Supreme Court buildings are in Bloemfontein. The map on page 101 locates these capitals.

QUICK CHECK

Summarize What is the name of South Africa's legislative branch?

Check Understanding

1. **VOCABULARY** Use the vocabulary words to write a paragraph about forming a new government.
   checks and balances
   environment

2. **READING SKILL** Summarize Use your chart from page 108 to write a summary of South Africa's government.

3. **Write About It** How can people in South Africa change their government?

VOCABULARY

agriculture p. 115

cash crops p. 115

livestock p. 115

READING SKILL

Summarize
Use the chart below to summarize what you learn about South Africa's economy.

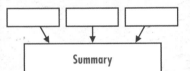

Summary

South Africa at Work

Ships come into the harbor of Durban, South Africa. A harbor is a sheltered place along the coast where ships can dock.

VISUAL PREVIEW

How do people affect the economy of South Africa?

A People mine gold, diamonds, and other minerals.

B Today, new job opportunities exist for all South Africans.

C Farmers use limited farmland to raise animals and crops for money.

D South Africa's culture and natural beauty make tourism a big business.

SELLING TO OTHER COUNTRIES

What do you want to be when you grow up? If you lived in South Africa, you might say, "I want to be a miner." That is hard work!

South Africa is not very big. Yet it is very important to Africa's economy. South Africa creates over 25 percent of Africa's wealth. It has 40 percent of all the businesses on the entire continent. South Africa exports many things to other countries. Since apartheid ended, more countries are buying South Africa's products.

Mining

More than half the money South Africa makes in exports comes from mining. Nearly half a million people have jobs mining gold, diamonds, copper, platinum, silver, and other minerals.

▲ Americans use the dollar. South Africans use the rand. Each rand is a different color.

QUICK CHECK

Summarize **What minerals does South Africa export to make money?**

Workers use trucks to dig copper mines. ▶

ⓑ WORKING IN FACTORIES

South Africa has many factories. Some make things that people can drive: trains, cars, or ships. The car your family drives may have some parts made in South Africa. Other factories make things that are used at home: computers, clothing, or processed foods. Still other factories make things like steel, iron, and other metal products.

New Chances

Under apartheid, many black South Africans did not have a chance for an education. They are studying now so they can get good jobs in factories and companies. Since apartheid ended, many companies from other countries have come to South Africa. They have created new jobs.

▲ Car manufacturing is a big industry in South Africa. Cars and trucks make up seven percent of South Africa's exports.

QUICK CHECK

Summarize **What things are made in South Africa's factories?**

▼ Many South Africans work in factories. This factory worker is making a product out of sandstone. Sandstone is a rock made up of grains of sand.

C FARMING THE LAND

South Africans also make money in **agriculture**. Agriculture is the business of growing crops and raising animals.

Crops for Money

Only a small amount of land in South Africa is good for farming. Farmers there raise crops for money. These are called **cash crops**. Their biggest cash crop is corn. Farmers also raise chickens, eggs, and apples.

Farmers raise animals for their meat and skins, too. Animals raised on farms and ranches are called **livestock**. These products are shipped all over the world.

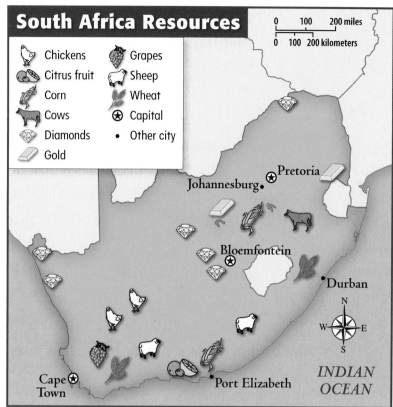

South Africa Resources

Chickens		Grapes	
Citrus fruit		Sheep	
Corn		Wheat	
Cows		⊛ Capital	
Diamonds		• Other city	
Gold			

0   100   200 miles
0   100   200 kilometers

Pretoria
Johannesburg
Bloemfontein
Durban
Cape Town
Port Elizabeth
INDIAN OCEAN

Map Skill

LOCATION **Where are grapes grown?**

QUICK CHECK

Summarize **What do South African farmers export?**

Ostriches are big birds that cannot fly. They are raised on ranches for their meat and skin, which is made into a strong leather. ▼

You learned that South Africans work many different jobs, just like Americans. One big job is helping tourists.

Helping Tourists

The business of helping tourists in a country is called tourism. Many tourists come to see South Africa's animals and parks. On a boat ride at the Greater St. Lucia Wetlands Park, you might see a hippo near the lily pads or a crocodile swimming by.

Tourists also visit places like Shakaland. There, they see Zulu dances and eat Zulu foods. You read about the Zulus in Lesson 1. Re-created communities like Shakaland are a good way to learn about how some South Africans live.

▲ This Zulu woman is wearing traditional Zulu dress. Tourists visit Shakaland to learn about Zulu culture.

After apartheid, many more tourists come to South Africa. They like to go on safaris. ▼

▲ Camps Bay is a beach in Cape Town. Many tourists go there in the summer, which is from November to March!

Jobs in Tourism

South Africans have jobs in nature parks, at beaches, at hotels, and in re-created communities. They work as tour guides, game wardens, servers, taxi drivers, and more.

Airports also provide many jobs. O. R. Tambo International Airport near Johannesburg is the busiest airport in all of Africa. You can fly nonstop from New York to Johannesburg, but it takes 15 hours!

QUICK CHECK

Summarize **How do South Africans earn money from tourism?**

Check Understanding

1. **VOCABULARY** Use the vocabulary words below to write an e-mail from a trip to South Africa.

   cash crops   **agriculture**

   livestock

2. **READING SKILL Summarize** Use your chart from page 112 to write a summary of South Africa's economy.

 3. **Write About It** Write a paragraph about how South Africa's economy is changing.

Use Line Graphs

VOCABULARY

line graph

One mineral mined in South Africa is platinum, a gray metal used in jewelry. To find out how much the price of platinum changed over the past 45 years, a **line graph** could show the information clearly. A line graph shows information that changes over time. You can also use more than one line graph to compare two different things.

Learn It

Look at the graph on this page as you follow the steps below.

- Read the graph title and labels to find out what the graph shows. The label on the left shows the price of platinum. The dates along the bottom show the years being tracked. This graph shows the changes in the price of platinum from 1960 to 2006.

- Look at the dots to see information for the years shown. In 1980, for example, platinum sold for close to $700 per ounce.

- Trace the lines connecting the dots to see changes over time.

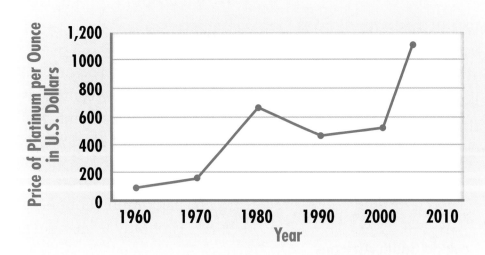

Price of Platinum, 1960–2006

Cape Town City Hall

Try It

Now look at the graph below.

- What type of graph is this?

- What does this graph show?

- What is the average monthly temperature in Cape Town in July?

- Does the temperature in Cape Town go up or down between August and December?

Apply It

Make a line graph to show information about a third-grade class that had a reading contest.

- In the first week, the blue team read 10 books and the yellow team read 12 books. In the second week, the blue team read 15 books and the yellow team read 15 books. In the third week, the blue team read 17 books and the yellow team read 20 books.

- What title will you give your graph?

- What information will you put along the bottom of your graph? What will you put along the side?

- In which week did the class read the most books?

- What does the graph show about the blue team and the yellow team?

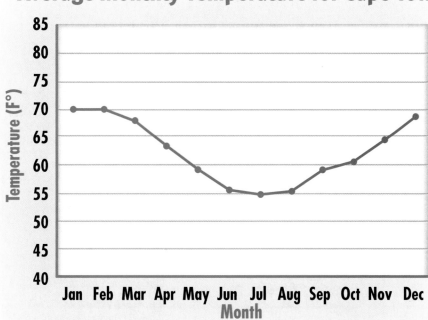

Average Monthly Temperature for Cape Town

Living in SOUTH AFRICA

Lesson 5

VOCABULARY

tournament p. 124

international p. 125

READING SKILL

Summarize

Use the chart below to summarize what you learn about life in South Africa.

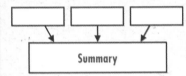

↓ ↓ ↓

Summary

New York Academic Content Standards

2.1, 2.2, 2.3, 2.4

Children in South Africa are just like you! They go to school, read, and have fun.

VISUAL PREVIEW

What is it like to live in South Africa?

A Johannesburg and Durban have become busy cities in South Africa.

B Cape Town is a city with many historic and modern places to see and visit.

C People in South Africa enjoy many activities in their free time.

A TWO EXCITING CITIES

Just like the United States, South Africa has exciting cities and towns. Johannesburg and Durban are South Africa's largest cities.

Johannesburg is South Africa's largest city. More than three million people live there. Turn back to page 101 and locate Johannesburg and Durban on the map. How would you describe their locations?

Johannesburg

Johannesburg is a busy city. It has its own sports teams and an orchestra. It is the home of MuseuMAfricA, a museum that tells about the history of Africa. It contains books, art, and musical instruments. The Apartheid Museum is also in Johannesburg. It describes the history of apartheid.

Durban

Durban is South Africa's second-largest city. It is located on the coast of the Indian Ocean. Durban is known for its beautiful beaches. Many tourists visit Durban each year.

▼ MuseuMAfricA is in Johannesburg.

QUICK CHECK

Summarize What are Johannesburg and Durban known for?

B CAPE TOWN

Cape Town is a very popular place in South Africa for tourists. It is also a historic city.

Cape Town is where Nelson Mandela gave his first speech after being released from prison. It was also home to an important medical event. In 1967 Dr. Christiaan Barnard did the first heart transplant on a person. A transplant is moving a body part from one body to another.

Castle of Good Hope

This is the Castle of Good Hope, the oldest building in Cape Town. Finished in 1679, it reminds us that Dutch traders settled Cape Town in 1652. There they met the Khoikhoi people.

Company Gardens

The Company Gardens have a statue of Cecil Rhodes. By the late 1800s, Rhodes controlled the diamond mines. He was one of the world's richest people. He set up a scholarship for college students called the Rhodes scholarship.

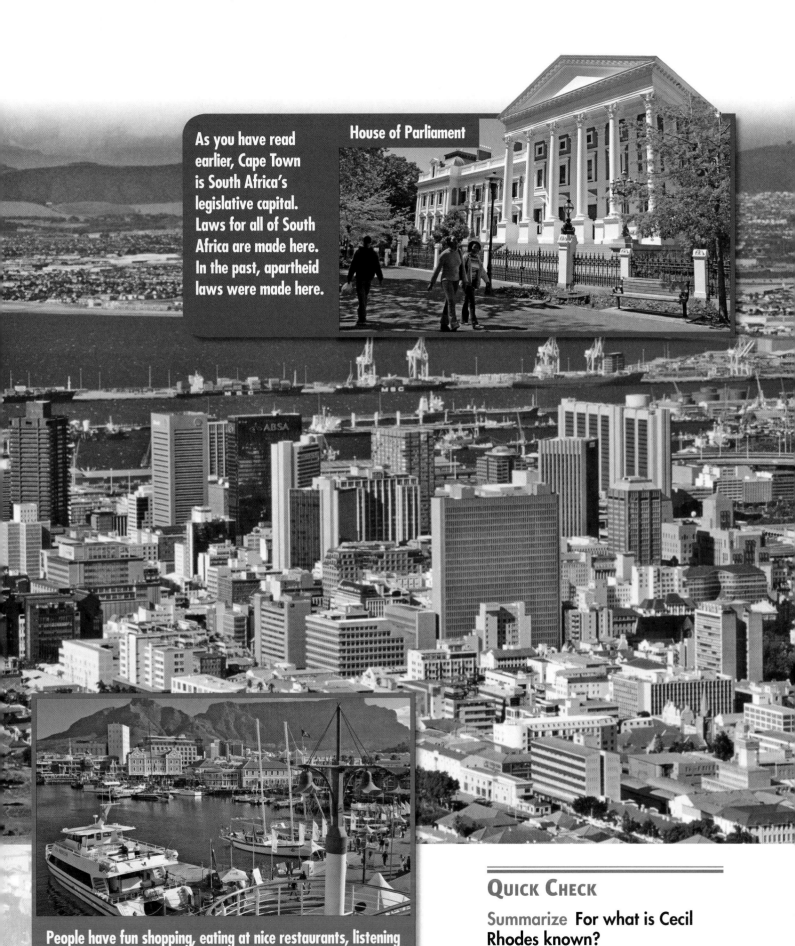

House of Parliament

As you have read earlier, Cape Town is South Africa's legislative capital. Laws for all of South Africa are made here. In the past, apartheid laws were made here.

People have fun shopping, eating at nice restaurants, listening to music, and dancing at the Victoria and Alfred Waterfront.

QUICK CHECK

Summarize **For what is Cecil Rhodes known?**

▲ If you hike up to the top of Table Mountain, you can see all of Cape Town below.

▲ South Africans enjoy playing a sport called cricket. Cricket is similar to baseball.

C FUN IN SOUTH AFRICA

Do you like to play sports? South Africans love playing rugby and cricket. Rugby is a sport like football, and cricket is a sport like baseball. They also play soccer. In 2010 South Africa will host the World Cup, the biggest men's soccer **tournament** in the world. A tournament is a series of games. A big, new soccer stadium is being built in Cape Town to hold all the fans!

Hiking

South Africans also love to hike. Many people enjoy hiking up Table Mountain in Cape Town. It takes about three hours.

PLACES

There is a beautiful neighborhood in Cape Town called Bo-Kaap. Its streets are lined with brightly-colored homes and buildings.

Bo-Kaap

Music

Like you, people in South Africa enjoy music. The Cape Town **International** Jazz Festival is a big gathering of jazz musicians. International means that it features musicians from many countries. The festival happens every March, during South Africa's summer. Thousands of South Africans and tourists go to the festival each year.

Cape Peninsula

If you like animals, Cape Peninsula is the place for you. A peninsula is a piece of land bordered by water on three sides. Cape Peninsula has rocky mountains, beautiful beaches, fishing villages, and lots of animals. Lucky visitors see groups of penguins marching along Boulders Beach.

QUICK CHECK

Summarize What are some fun things people do in Cape Town?

▲ People in South Africa take part in many carnivals and parades, such as this one in Cape Town.

Check Understanding

1. **VOCABULARY** Write a postcard to a friend about a visit to Cape Town. Use the vocabulary words below.
tournament   **international**

2. **READING SKILL** Summarize Use the chart from page 120 to write a summary of life in South Africa.

3. **Write About It** Write a paragraph about how South Africa's cities have changed.

Unit 3 Review and Assess

Vocabulary

Number a paper from 1 to 5. Write the word from the list below that matches the description.

apartheid   veld   safari

Boer   agriculture

1. wide, flat areas covered in grass

2. the business of growing crops and raising animals

3. a trip to an African game reserve

4. a Dutch settler of South Africa

5. the official South African policy of separating people by race

Comprehension and Critical Thinking

6. What are some natural resources South Africa gets from its land?

7. Why did the Dutch settle in Cape Town in 1652?

8. What are the three branches of South Africa's government?

9. **Reading Skill** Why did South Africa need a new constitution after the end of apartheid?

10. **Critical Thinking** Why might Cape Town be a good place to live?

Skill

Use Line Graphs

Write a complete sentence to answer each question.

11. Why are line graphs useful?

12. Study the line graph on the right. Between which months is the temperature in Cape Town the same as the temperature in Cairo?

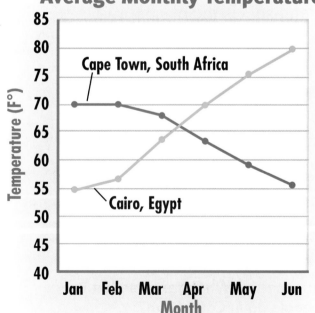

Average Monthly Temperature

New York English Language Arts Test Preparation

Directions

Read this passage about South Africa's national flower. Then answer questions 1 and 2.

South Africa's national flower is the king protea. The flower can be found in the southwestern and southern areas of the Western Cape. The king protea looks a lot like an artichoke. The bloom can be up to 12 inches across. Tourists come from all over the world to see the flowers in bloom.

The flower was named for the Greek God Proteus, who could adapt to almost anything. The flower is fighting to survive through climate change and development. Up to 60 percent of the proteas will be extinct by 2050.

---

1 What is happening to the protea?

  A It is spreading north.

  B It is becoming extinct.

  C It is no longer the national flower.

  D It is being sold.

2 Why was the protea named after the Greek god Proteus?

  A It came from Greece.

  B It can adapt.

  C It is a new type of flower.

  D It looks like an artichoke.

The Big Idea Activities

How do people change the place where they live?

Write About the Big Idea

Narrative Paragraph

Think about the changes you read about in Unit 3. What it would have been like to live through all of the change in South Africa? Use your Foldable to help you write an essay that answers the Big Idea question, "How do people change the place where they live?" Your paragraph should summarize how you would view living in South Africa, using the information you recorded in your Foldable.

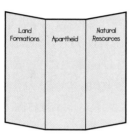

Draw a Picture of a Landform in South Africa

Go back and read lesson 2 again. Pick the landform of South Africa that was most interesting to you. Draw a picture of the landform and label it. Then write two or three sentences describing your picture.

After your picture is finished, compare your picture to that of a classmate who picked the same landform that you did. How are your pictures different? How are they similar? What did he or she write about?

The teacher will collect all the pictures and post them on a bulletin board. Are there pictures of all of South Africa's landforms mentioned in the lesson?

South Africa's Coast

Unit 4

EXPLORE The Big Idea

Essential Question
How do people in a country meet their needs?

FOLDABLES™ Study Organizer

Cause and Effect
Make a Folded Table to take notes on life in Italy as you read Unit 4. Label the columns **Geography**, **History**, **Government**, and **Economics**.

Geography	History	Government	Economics

LOG ON
For more about Unit 4 go to
www.macmillanmh.com

Many of Italy's towns grew into powerful cities because of their central location on the Mediterranean Sea.

ITALY:
The OLD and the NEW

PEOPLE, PLACES, and EVENTS

Julius Caesar

The Roman Forum

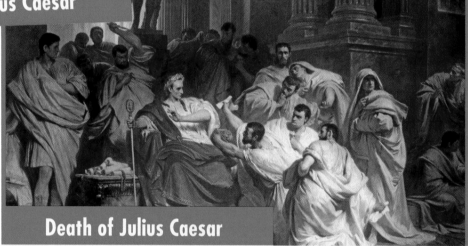

Death of Julius Caesar

44 B.C. Julius Caesar was murdered by some senators who did not agree with the way he ruled and thought he had become too powerful.

Julius Caesar was a general who became a Roman leader. He was **murdered** in the Senate House in the **Forum**, an open area with many buildings.

Today you can walk through the Forum in Rome and see the reconstructed Senate House.

LOG ON

For more about People, Places, and Events visit
www.macmillanmh.com

Isabella d'Este

Mantua

Isabella Holds Court

1500s

Isabella helped many writers and artists. They would meet in her palace and share their art.

Isabella d'Este lived during the Renaissance, a time of great art and culture in Italy. She was married to the ruler of **Mantua** and later became its ruler.

Today you can travel to Mantua and see the **palace** where she lived. You can visit its many rooms and gardens.

Lesson 1

VOCABULARY

peninsula p. 133

ruin p. 133

mountainous p. 134

port p. 137

village p. 138

READING SKILL

Cause and Effect
Copy the chart below.
List how people use the
land of Italy.

Cause	→	Effect
	→	
	→	
	→	

New York Academic Content Standards

3.1, 3.2, 4.1

The Land of ITALY

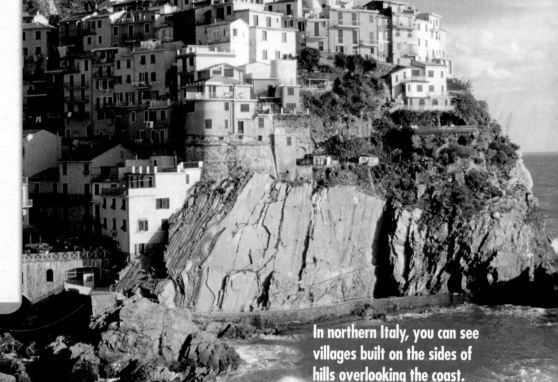

In northern Italy, you can see villages built on the sides of hills overlooking the coast.

VISUAL PREVIEW

How does the land of Italy help people live?

A Italy has busy cities in the north and agriculture in the south.

B People hike the mountains and grow food in the hills and valleys.

C Italians use the water that is all around their country for work and play.

D People in Italy live in cities, towns, and villages.

A FOOT IN TWO WORLDS

Italy is easy to find on a map because of its shape. Many people think it looks like a tall boot with a high heel! What do you think it looks like?

Italy is a **peninsula**, a long stretch of land with water all around it. It is both a part of Europe and in the center of the Mediterranean Sea, not far from Africa.

▲ Italy's land is good for growing grapes.

North and South

The northern part of Italy borders other countries in Southern Europe. They are divided by a natural border, the famous mountain range called the Alps. Many of Italy's cities and major businesses are located in the north. The foot of the boot, the southern area of Italy, is more agricultural. It once belonged to Greece, and you can still see Greek **ruins** there! A ruin is an old building that has fallen apart over time.

Map Skill

LOCATION Which countries border Italy?

QUICK CHECK

Cause and Effect **Why are the Greek buildings in Italy ruins?**

HILLS, MOUNTAINS AND PLAINS

Some of the land in Italy is **mountainous**. It is steep and rocky. Other parts of Italy are hilly. There are many plains. This land is good for farming and raising animals.

Hills

Many towns are built on hillsides. The capital city of Rome is built over seven hills. When you travel through the rolling hills of Tuscany, you can see cypress trees and crops growing.

Mountain Ranges

The Apennines are a long chain of mountains. They run all along the Italian boot. This mountain range has forests and wildlife. It is a good place to go hiking.

The Alps are found in northern Italy. Many people go to the Alpine slopes to ski. Hiking in the mountains is a way to see flowers and animals that are unique to Italy.

A skier in the Italian Alps ▼

From a town in Tuscany, you can get a good view of the countryside. ▼

▲ The Po River runs through the center of the Po River Valley.

▲ Mt. Etna can be seen from a site of Roman ruins in Sicily.

Po River Valley

The Po River valley is Italy's largest flat area of land. It is located between the Alps and Apennines. Many crops are grown on its rich land, including grapes and olives.

Islands

Two islands are part of Italy. They are called Sardinia and Sicily. Sardinia is at the knee of the boot. Sicily is at the toe of the boot. Today Sicily is part of Italy. It is known for its bright art, good cooking, and lively music. Sicily is a mountainous island. Its biggest mountain is a volcano called Etna. Most people on these islands speak Italian. However, they speak it with a different accent. They sound so different that sometimes other Italians have trouble understanding them!

QUICK CHECK

Cause and Effect Why are crops grown in the Po River valley?

PLACES

Inside Italy is a tiny nation called San Marino. At only 24 square miles in area, San Marino is nearly the same size as Manhattan in New York City. San Marino has been a separate country for thousands of years. People in San Marino speak Italian.

San Marino

C WATER, WATER EVERYWHERE!

Italians use the water around them for fun and for work. Italy has more than 4,000 miles of coastline. A coastline is the place where land meets the water of an ocean or sea. Italy's coastline and rivers have a big impact on how people live.

The Rivers

There are many good rivers in Italy. Many are wide and calm. Farmers can use the rivers to ship their goods. This is important because towns along the rivers can get goods from many miles away. Rome and Florence are cities that were built on rivers.

▲ The Ponte Vecchio bridge on the Arno River in Florence was built in medieval times.

▼ Venice is built in the water. The roads in its center are canals. People travel on boats and water buses called vaporettos!

▲ Fishermen in Genoa prepare for a day of activity.

◀ The harbor of Genoa is still active today. Christopher Columbus was born in Genoa.

Italy's Coastline

Some parts of the coastline have good beaches. People go there to play in the sand and water. Other areas are rocky and dangerous. Some people visit these places because of their beauty.

There are important towns along the coast called **ports**. A port is a place where boats can bring their goods to land. Ships from all over the world enter busy ports. Many fishermen from large and small ports go to sea every day. The seafaring life has been a part of Italian history for years.

QUICK CHECK

Cause and Effect **How do people use the water in Venice?**

D PEOPLE LIVING ON THE LAND

Italy is not enormous, but it is full of people. Italy has about 58 million people. They live in towns, large cities, and small **villages**.

Italian Towns

Many people in Italy live in small towns. There are many towns in the middle part of Italy. They have houses, churches, and schools.

Big Cities

The northern part of Italy has the most people. There you can find many of Italy's cities. People move to the cities to find good jobs. Italian cities are like big cities in America. They have tall buildings and many cars. They have apartment buildings and parks where people live and play. Many cities have subways and trains.

▲ Italians buy fresh fruit and other foods in a market.

The Galleria Vittorio Emanuele II in Milan is one of the first shopping malls. ▼

▲ The piazza is a public area where people can meet each other and relax.

Small Villages

The southern part of Italy has many small villages. The people who live there are often farmers. This part of Italy has rolling green hills. The houses are not close together.

People who live in villages must travel a long way to get to a city. That is why they often make or grow their own food. Sometimes a busy city person likes to visit a village. It is a good place to slow down and relax.

QUICK CHECK

Cause and Effect Why do people in the south often grow their own food?

Check Understanding

1. **VOCABULARY** Write four sentences that tell what you learned about Italy. Use the vocabulary words below.

   mountainous   peninsula
   village   port

2. **READING SKILLS Cause and Effect** Use your chart from page 132 to show how Italy's coastline affects the people of Italy.

3. **Write About It** How is the land in the northern part of Italy different from the land in the southern part?

Map and Globe Skills

Use A Road Map

VOCABULARY

mountain pass

tunnel

road map

A **mountain pass** is a steep road over a mountain. It is usually a long, winding road. When it snows, mountain passes can be dangerous. However, the people in Italy solved the problem. They build **tunnels** under the mountains. A tunnel is a wide road for cars and trucks. If you drove in Italy, you would need a **road map** to help you find the tunnels.

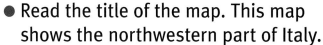

Learn It

Look at the map on page 141. Follow the steps for reading a road map.

- Read the title of the map. This map shows the northwestern part of Italy.

- Find the key on the map. This will help you understand the symbols.

- Identify the different kinds of roads. Find the highway, main roads, and tunnels on the map.

- Just like in the United States, roads in Italy have numbers. The numbers are marked on the map. Each road has a different number.

◄ The Mont Blanc Tunnel was constructed by teams who drilled the tunnel under the mountain Mont Blanc.

Northwest Italy

Map labels: SWITZERLAND, Europe, A1, A2, A13, A9, A40, A41, SS33, SS36, SS42, Chamonix, Mont Blanc, SS27, A5, SS536, Courmayeur, A L P S, A26, A8, A9, A4, N90, A5, A4, A26, Milan, SS415, A43, A4, A7, A21, A1, A32, N91, SS23, Turin, A21, A21, SS231, I T A L Y, SS45, FRANCE, A7, SS21, SS231, A26, A15, SS20, A6, Genoa, A12, A10, Mediterranean Sea

Legend:
— International boundary
⟩•••⟨ Tunnel
═ Highway
━ Main road
• City
▲ Mountain peak

0 — 20 — 40 miles
0 — 20 — 40 kilometers

Try It

Use the map above to answer the questions.

- How many tunnels can you find on the map?

- What mountain range does the Mont Blanc tunnel go under?

- What highway would you take to reach Milan from Genoa?

Apply It

Find a road map of your town or state. What are the roads near you? Are they highways or main roads?

Lesson 2

VOCABULARY

empire p. 143

city-state p. 146

patron p. 146

renaissance p. 147

READING SKILL

Cause and Effect

Copy the chart below. List how events in history changed Italy.

Cause	→	Effect
	→	
	→	
	→	

New York Academic Content Standards

2.1, 2.2, 2.3, 2.4

The History of ITALY

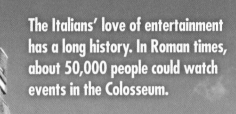

The Italians' love of entertainment has a long history. In Roman times, about 50,000 people could watch events in the Colosseum.

VISUAL PREVIEW

How did people live at different times in Italian history?

A Ancient Italy was settled by peoples such as the Greeks and Romans.

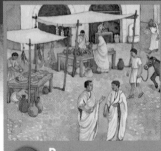

B Roman emperors controlled a large empire.

C Italy was the center of the Renaissance.

A ITALY IN ANCIENT TIMES

Have you ever gone to a big stadium to see a sports event? Thousands of years ago, a great stadium was built in Rome. It was called the Colosseum. Part of it is still standing today.

Many Greeks settled in Italy. They brought their religion and culture with them. Other people in Italy, such as the Romans, learned new ideas from them.

▲ This Roman mask protected its wearer's face.

Growth of Rome

The Roman people built the city of Rome. The power of Rome grew. Its leaders were strong, and they built large armies. Soldiers were well trained and brave. They conquered many lands. Soon, the Romans ruled most of Italy. Generals such as Julius Caesar brought more land under Roman control. These areas became known as the Roman **Empire**. An empire is a group of lands that is led by an emperor or king. Much of the Roman Empire bordered on the Mediterranean Sea.

QUICK CHECK

Cause and Effect **What caused Rome to become an empire?**

A Roman soldier, called a legionnaire, used a spear and shield. ▶

THE AMAZING ROMAN EMPIRE

The first Roman emperor, Augustus, improved life in the Roman Empire by building roads, buildings, and water systems. Today in Italy, we can still see many things that remain from this time, even though they are about 2,000 years old!

All Roads Lead to Rome

For hundreds of years, Rome had been an important center. During the time of the Roman Empire, about one million people lived in Rome. The city of Rome was an exciting place to visit. Farmers and merchants traveled there to do business. Senators and scholars could be seen in conversation in its public squares.

The people of ancient Italy loved to go to the baths, which were like warm swimming pools. They brought water in from faraway streams.

Rich people were carried in litters through the streets.

Roads in the empire were good and kept the lands connected. Some of these roads still exist today.

The Romans invented concrete and used it to build temples and other grand buildings.

The Romans even had a mail delivery system! Messengers traveled in wagons led by horses.

Farmers grew food and sold it in the city.

QUICK CHECK

Cause and Effect **How did roads help the Romans?**

◀ In his painting "The School of Athens", Italian artist Raphael, shows famous Greek teachers.

C   A GREAT TIME FOR THE ARTS

The power of the Roman Empire did not last. Its lands were divided. During the Middle Ages, some Italian cities grew into **city-states**. A city-state is a city that governs itself.

Life in the City-States

Many of the city-states, such as Venice and Florence, were in northern Italy. Each city-state had its own rulers. Many of these rulers loved the arts and were **patrons**. A patron is a person who supports art. Patrons gave artists money and a place to live. An important patron was Isabella d'Este, who lived in Mantua.

▲ Da Vinci's drawing for a flying machine

PEOPLE

Leonardo da Vinci is called a "Renaissance Man" because of his many talents. He painted and designed buildings. He studied the human body like a scientist. He played music. He also drew plans for new inventions, such as a submarine.

Leonardo da Vinci

This church in Florence was built during the Renaissance. Its dome was designed by the architect Brunelleschi. It was considered a major engineering feat. ▶

Learning from Ancient Times

In the 1300s and 1400s, people in Italy began to study ancient Greek and Roman culture again. This period was later called the **Renaissance**. The word renaissance means "rebirth." This word is used for the period because parts of Italy's ancient culture were reborn. Renaissance artists in Italy also created new kinds of art and architecture. Italian painting influenced art in other places.

Modern Italy

For many centuries, Italy's lands were ruled by different rulers and countries. Its people decided that they wanted a country with one ruler. In the 1800s, Italy was united and led by a king. By 1946 Italians saw that they needed a new government. They chose to have a democracy, like the United States. They celebrate this change on Republic Day, which is June 2.

QUICK CHECK

Cause and Effect **How did having a patron help an artist?**

Check Understanding

1. **VOCABULARY** Describe what you learned about Italy. Use the vocabulary words below.

   empire   renaissance

   patron   city-state

2. **READING SKILLS Cause and Effect** Use your chart from page 143. Explain what caused the Renaissance in Italy.

3. **Write About It** What were two important periods in Italy's history? Describe them in a short paragraph.

VOCABULARY

council p. 149

cabinet p. 151

READING SKILL

Cause and Effect
Copy the chart below. List how Italians select their leaders.

Cause	→	Effect
	→	
	→	
	→	

New York Academic Content Standards
2.1, 2.2, 2.3, 2.4, 5.1, 5.2, 5.4

Governing ITALY

This former palace in Rome houses the Chamber of Deputies.

VISUAL PREVIEW

How does Italy's government meet the needs of its people?

A Italians decided to be ruled by elected leaders.

B Italy has a president, parliament, prime minister, and cabinet.

Ⓐ CHOOSING LEADERS

Have you ever heard the names Veneto, Umbria, and Lazio? These are some of the regions in Italy. Regions are like states. Italy has twenty regions.

Each state in America has its own name. It also has its own leaders. Italy is very similar.

Voting for Leaders

In 1946 Italians voted to be led by a president instead of a king. Since then, they have elected their leaders. Just as in the United States, the people in each region vote for their leaders. The result of the vote shows who will be the leader of the region. The leaders of each region in Italy are called a **council**. The council makes laws and tries to solve the problems of the region.

QUICK CHECK

Cause and Effect What happened when Italians no longer wanted to be ruled by a king?

In Italy, votes are placed in portable voting boxes. ▶

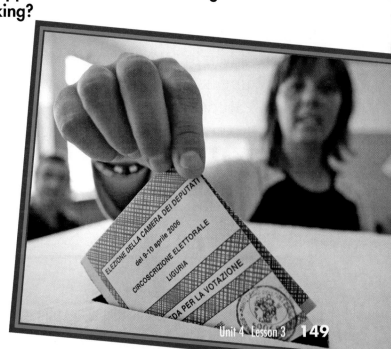

▲ The Senate meets in Rome.

Citizenship

Visiting the Capital

As in the United States, the country's leaders work and live in its capital city. Rome, the ancient capital, was declared the capital once again in 1871. Another name for Rome is the "parliamentary city." Students from all parts of Italy travel to see laws being discussed in the Chamber of Deputies.

Write About It What are reasons to visit a capital city?

Some laws are made for the whole country. Just as in the United States, Italy has national leaders and bodies of government.

The President

You probably know that Americans elect a president every four years. A president is the leader of a nation. Italy also has a president. The president is elected every seven years.

The Parliament

The parliament in Italy is the group of people who make the laws. Like the president, they are elected. There are leaders from every region in Parliament. It is made up of two parts, the Senate and the Chamber of Deputies. Just as in the United States, the leaders in Parliament sometimes disagree. People from the farming regions do not always like the laws that are good for the cities. The leaders must work together. They try to make good laws for all Italians.

Prime Minister Romano Prodi and President Giorgio Napolitano meet with women ministers.

The Prime Minister and the Cabinet

In Italy, the president names a person to be the prime minister. This does not happen in the United States. A prime minister is the leader of Parliament. He talks to the president and the cabinet about how to solve problems.

Leaders need help making decisions. In both Italy and the United States, a group of experts give advice. These people are called the **cabinet**. In the United States, the cabinet advises the president. In Italy, it is headed by the prime minister and is called the Council of Ministers.

QUICK CHECK

Cause and Effect **Why do leaders in parliament have to work together?**

Check Understanding

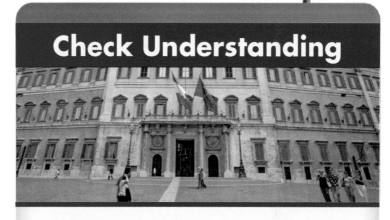

1. **VOCABULARY** Write a sentence using each of the words below.
   cabinet   council

2. **READING SKILL Cause and Effect** Use your chart from page 148 to explain how the people play a part in the government of Italy.

Cause	→	Effect
	→	
	→	
	→	

3. **Write About It** Explain how the Italian government is different from the government in the United States.

Lesson 4

VOCABULARY

designer p. 155

resort p. 157

READING SKILL

Cause and Effect
Copy the chart below.
List the effects of the jobs
people have in Italy

Cause	→	Effect
	→	
	→	
	→	

New York Academic Content Standards
3.1, 3.2, 4.1, 4.2

Italy at Work

In the hilly parts of Italy, farmers grow
grapes and olives on small plots of land.

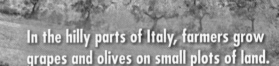

VISUAL PREVIEW

How do people affect Italy's economy?

A Farmers raise animals and grow crops to make cheese, wine, and oils.

B Craftsmen and designers create fine goods that are sold around the world.

C Visitors spend money to see the sights and to enjoy many activities.

A   A TASTE OF ITALY

Have you ever eaten spaghetti, nougat, or gelato? These foods came to the United States from Italy! We also buy food items made in Italy, such as cheese, tomatoes, and olives.

Italian olives are used to make olive oil. Grapes are used to make Italian wine that is famous all over the world. The milk from cows makes cheese. Did you know that Mozzarella cheese comes from Italy?

▲ Mozzarella cheese made from buffalo milk is an Italian specialty.

Small Farms, Big Jobs

Most of Italy is too rocky or hilly for farming. Therefore, most Italian farms are small. Farmers also raise sheep and cows on the hillsides. The plains in the Po River Valley have larger, more modern farms.

The Mediterranean Sea surrounds Italy. It helps keep the weather mild all year round. That means good weather for farming, especially in the south. Farmers have a long time to grow their crops. Some of the best olive oil, cheeses, and wines are made in the south.

A worker in a cheese shop removes cheeses from their molds. ▼

QUICK CHECK

Cause and Effect Why is mild weather good for farmers?

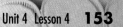

 MAKING ITALIAN GOODS

Italians are very creative. You can see this in their home-cooked dishes or mass-produced cars. Many of the goods made in Italy are popular in other countries. People all over the world buy Italian wine, shoes, and clothing. This keeps Italy's economy strong.

Beautifully patterned silks are made today in Italian silk factories. ▼

Fine olive oil is still made in the old-fashioned way. The olives are crushed. Then the liquid oil is separated from the solids in an olive press.

Hand-painted pottery is produced in Tuscany and other parts of Italy.

The violin was invented in Italy in the 1500s. Violins are still made in Italy. This instrument maker is finishing a violin by adding a layer of varnish to it.

Italian Crafts and Fine Design

Italians have a long tradition in crafts. Different places in Italy produce special wares. Glassblowing, making handmade paper, and even forming the many shapes of pasta take great skill! Italian **designers** are known for their exciting style and well-made products. A designer is a person who makes a plan for creating something. Italian shoes, cars, and handbags are all fine products made in Italy.

Handmade pasta is hung up to dry in a pasta factory in Naples.

Italy is known for its leatherwork, such as these shoes.

QUICK CHECK

Cause and Effect **Why do people all over the world want to buy goods from Italy?**

People from all over the world visit Italy. They are called tourists. A tourist is a person who travels for pleasure. Tourism is good for Italy's economy. Some tourists like to visit ancient buildings and ruins. Rome is a good place for them. Others like to see great Italian art. They enjoy the museums in Florence.

DataGraphic
Tourism Helps the Economy

Study the pictograph and bar graph below. Answer the questions that follow.

World's Most Popular Tourism Spots, 2004

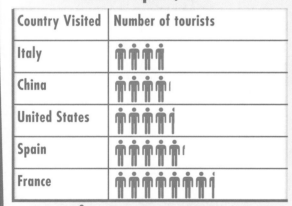

Country Visited	Number of tourists
Italy	🧍🧍🧍🧍
China	🧍🧍🧍🧍ı
United States	🧍🧍🧍🧍🧍ı
Spain	🧍🧍🧍🧍🧍ı
France	🧍🧍🧍🧍🧍🧍🧍🧍ı

🧍 = 10 million tourists

Tourism Earnings, 2004

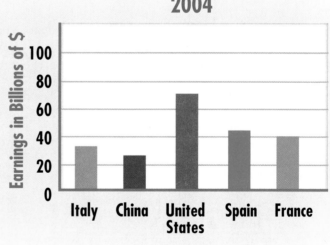

Think About Tourism and the Economy

1. Which country brought in the most money from tourism in 2004?

2. About how many tourists visited Italy in 2004?

▲ An exciting event to catch is the Palio Festival. You can watch a horse race and medieval flag-waving!

Enjoy Life with the Italians!

Many Italians spend their vacations in their own country. They go skiing in the mountains. They go to the beaches. They sometimes visit the beautiful islands, Sicily and Sardinia. Italy's long coast draws many visitors. They come to swim. They go boating. They stay at beach **resorts** in towns along the coast. A resort is a special hotel for tourists. There are also many celebrations throughout the year that visitors can enjoy.

QUICK CHECK

Cause and Effect **Why do many tourists come to Italy?**

Check Understanding

1. **VOCABULARY** Write an advertisement for tourists. Use the vocabulary words below
   designer   **resort**

2. **READING SKILL Cause and Effect** Use your chart from page 152 to write a paragraph about how the land of Italy affects the way people earn a living.

Cause	→	Effect
	→	
	→	
	→	

 EXPLORE The Big Idea
3. **Write About It** Write a list of the jobs people in Italy have.

Chart and Graph Skills

Use Flow Charts

VOCABULARY

flow chart

Have you ever wondered how cheese is made? Did you know that cheese starts out as milk? It goes through many steps before it becomes cheese. These steps have to be done in a certain order. A **flow chart** shows the different steps necessary to complete an activity. It can help you understand and remember the steps in the right order.

Making Parmesan Cheese

Learn It

Look at the chart to the right as you read about using a flow chart.

- Read the title of the chart. This flow chart shows the steps for turning milk into cheese.

- Look at the pictures and read the labels. Both the pictures and the labels give information.

- The arrows show the order of the steps. Read the steps in order and follow the arrows. You can see that the cheese must be aged before it is sold.

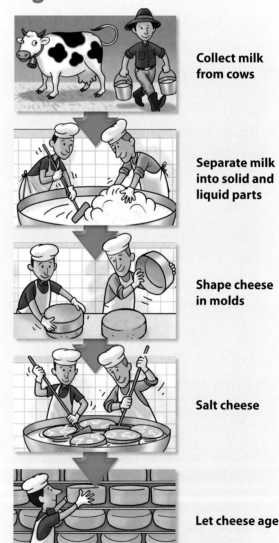

Collect milk from cows

Separate milk into solid and liquid parts

Shape cheese in molds

Salt cheese

Let cheese age

Answer the questions by reading the flow chart on this page.

● What does the chart show?

● How many steps are there in the activity? What is the first step? What is the last step?

● What does the flow chart tell you about how farmers get wool?

● What happens after the wool is spun?

Apply It

Think of a process that you know well. For example, do you know how to plant a tree or bake a cake? Make your own flow chart to show the steps in that process. Draw a picture for each step. Then write a label to go with each picture. Use arrows and numbers to show the order of the steps. Show how you do it with a flow chart.

Making Woolen Cloth

Shear wool from sheep

Clean wool

Spin yarn

Weave cloth

Dye woolen cloth

Lesson 5

VOCABULARY

extinct p. 163

opera p. 164

translated p. 165

marionette p. 165

READING SKILL

Cause and Effect
Copy the chart below. Use the chart to tell how culture affects families.

Cause	→	Effect
	→	
	→	
	→	

New York Academic Content Standards
2.1, 2.2, 2.3, 2.4, 3.1

Italians attend a musical event in an open air theater from Roman times.

VISUAL PREVIEW

How does the culture of Italy make it a special place?

A Italian families are close and share their traditions.

B Families in Naples enjoy a city rich with culture and history.

C Italians share their art, music, and stories with the world.

JOIN THE FAMILY

What do you most enjoy doing with your family?
Whether you live in a small town or big city,
you are part of a family and a community.

Just like American families, Italian families spend time together. They go to parks and to movies. Italian parents teach their children about their culture. Many travel together all over Italy.

Family Life

Italian families are close. They often live near their relatives. Some Italian families are very big. They have lots of aunts, uncles, and grandchildren. Families gather on weekends and holidays. They share celebrations all through the year. A big part of the celebrations is a home-cooked meal. On Sundays, many Italian families continue the tradition of a *passeggiata*, or taking a walk together.

QUICK CHECK

Cause and Effect **How do Italian families show they are close?**

Three generations of a family eat together. ▶

Naples has narrow streets as well as inviting piazzas.

Ⓑ NAPLES, CAPITAL OF THE SOUTH

If you have eaten pizza made with mozzarella cheese, tomato sauce, and basil, you have had Pizza Margherita. What do you think its colors represent? In the 1800s and 1900s, many Italians from Naples moved to the United States. They brought their traditions with them, like Pizza Margherita!

A City Full of History

The city of Naples is hundreds of years old. It was first settled by the Greeks long ago. Today, you can see ruins of Greek temples just south of Naples. Later the city was part of the Roman Empire. Its beautiful streets have grand buildings and monuments built by the many different people who lived there.

EVENT

The volcano Mount Vesuvius erupted in AD 79. Lava and ash destroyed the Roman city of Pompeii, located at the bottom of the mountain. It was frozen in time. When archaeologists dug up the city in the 1700s, they could imagine how it looked centuries earlier. They learned a lot about Roman life of the time.

Ruins in Pompeii

Located on the Mediterranean Sea, Naples is an important port city. The port bustles with people and merchants.

A Volcano for a Neighbor

If you lived in Naples, you would never be far from the volcano Mount Vesuvius. In most ways, the volcano is good for Naples. Tourists come to see it because it is beautiful. The soil on its slopes is rich. It is a good place to grow fruit and vines.

However, the volcano is not **extinct**. That means it will erupt again some day. The last time it erupted was in 1944. Today, scientists watch the volcano all the time. They warn the people in Naples if they hear rumblings.

QUICK CHECK

Cause and Effect How is Mount Vesuvius good for Naples?

Primary Sources

To see Naples as we saw it in the early dawn from far up on the side of Vesuvius, is to see a picture of wonderful beauty.

**Writer Mark Twain
from his book, *The Innocents Abroad***

Write About It Write a paragraph that describes how your own town or city looks.

Ships from all over the world come to the Bay of Naples with their goods.

Italy has a rich culture. Italians love the arts, and they continue to be interested in their artistic heritage. They also enjoy modern forms of entertainment.

Art All Around

Italian art is displayed in many museums. You can also see great artwork in buildings and public squares. Some churches and palaces have paintings that were painted directly onto the walls! In city plazas, you can see fountains and statues. Even many of the doors and walls of buildings are colorfully decorated.

The Gift of Music

Music is an important part of Italy's culture. One Italian who wrote music was Rossini. He explained how he could make music out of anything. He said: "Give me a laundry-list, and I'll set it to music!" Rossini and other Italian composers wrote a special form of music called **opera**. An opera is a musical work. It is a play performed on a stage, but all the players sing their lines. Italian operas are famous and are performed all over the world.

▲ The Trevi Fountain in Rome shows symbols of the sea.

Operas have grand sets and beautiful costumes. ▼

National Pride

Sports are popular in Italy. A great interest is soccer. Italy's national team has won the World Cup four times. Italy also often hosts ski events.

Storytelling, the Italian Way

Have you ever read about the **marionette** Pinocchio? A marionette is a puppet on strings. The original story was written by an Italian. When it was **translated** into English, it became very popular. To translate means to rewrite in another language.

Italians have written other great books. People all over the world read them. They also see Italian films, famous for their new ideas and high quality. Even if you live in the United States, you can enjoy a lot of Italian culture!

QUICK CHECK

Cause and Effect Why do we know the story of Pinocchio?

The story of Pinocchio was written by a man from Tuscany.

▲ The Italian soccer team celebrates winning the World Cup in 2006.

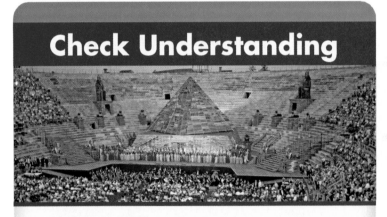

Check Understanding

1. **VOCABULARY** Write a poem about Italian culture. Use the vocabulary words.

   marionette   opera
   translated   extinct

2. **READING SKILL Cause and Effect** Use your chart from page 160. Tell how Mt. Vesuvius affects Naples.

Cause	→	Effect
	→	
	→	
	→	

3. **Write About It** How do Italians bring culture into their lives?

Unit 4 · Review and Assess

Vocabulary

Number a paper from 1 to 4. Beside each number write the word from the list below that matches the description.

cabinet   patron

marionette   peninsula

1. a puppet on a string
2. a group of experts who give advice
3. a long stretch of land surrounded by water
4. a person who supports an artist

Comprehension and Critical Thinking

5. Why is water so important in Italian life?
6. How did patrons help culture grow during the Renaissance?
7. What is the president's job in Italy?
8. **Reading Skill** What are some examples of products made in Italy?
9. **Critical Thinking** What is an opera, and why is it unique?

Skill

Use a Road Map

Write a complete sentence to answer each question.

10. What is the name of the tunnel that passes through the Alps?
11. What cities does this tunnel connect?

Mont Blanc Tunnel

Chamonix

FRANCE

N205

Mont Blanc Tunnel

A L P S

Mont Blanc

ITALY

Courmayeur

SS26

International boundary
Tunnel
Main road
City
Mountain peak

N
W E
S

0   1   2 miles
0   1   2 kilometers

New York English Language Arts Test Preparation

Directions

Read the following biography of Leonardo da Vinci. Then answer questions 1 through 3.

Leonardo da Vinci was good at many things. He was a painter, sculptor, engineer, architect, and inventor. He is famous for painting *The Last Supper* and the *Mona Lisa*. Leonardo was also interested in science and plants. He used what he learned from his studies to invent new things. His inventions include a clock, tank, flying machine, a helicopter, and a parachute. Leonardo da Vinci died in 1519. Leonardo is one of the most important figures of the Renaissance.

---

1 Read this sentence from the paragraph.

Leonardo was also interested in science and plants.

What does the word "interested" **most likely** mean in this sentence?

A liked

B disliked

C ignored

D hated

2 Based on his inventions, which of the following was Leonardo fascinated with?

A eating

B running

C flying

D swimming

3 The **main** idea of the biography is that _____.

A Leonardo was lazy

B Leonardo was too busy with painting to explore other things

C Leonardo was good at lots of things

D Leonardo's inventions were silly

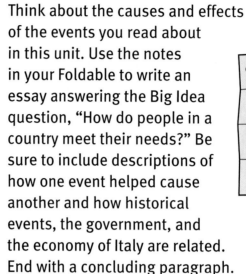

The Big Idea Activities

Write About the Big Idea

How do people in a country meet their needs?

Expository Essay

FOLDABLES
Study Organizer

Think about the causes and effects of the events you read about in this unit. Use the notes in your Foldable to write an essay answering the Big Idea question, "How do people in a country meet their needs?" Be sure to include descriptions of how one event helped cause another and how historical events, the government, and the economy of Italy are related. End with a concluding paragraph.

Geography	History	Government	Economics

Make a Picture Map of Italy

Work in pairs. Make a picture map of Italy that will teach someone traveling to Italy about places to visit. Here is how to make your map.

1. Choose one part of Italy that you want to focus on, such as a major city or island.

2. Look in books for maps, pictures, and facts about your place. Choose some sites in your city to include on your map.

3. Draw the shape of your place on a large piece of paper.

4. Place your own drawings or photos of important sites in the correct part of your place.

5. Label the drawings and photos and write the name of the place you chose.

China has both large, busy cities and small, quiet villages.

EXPLORE
The Big Idea

Unit 5

Essential Question
How do differences exist within and between communities?

FOLDABLES
Study Organizer

Compare and Contrast
Make a Three-Tab Book Foldable and label the tabs **Ancient**, **Both**, and **Modern**. Use this Foldable to take notes on how China's life, government, and economics are all both old and new.

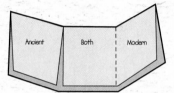

Ancient | Both | Modern

LOG ON
For more about Unit 5 go to
www.macmillanmh.com

CHINA
A Land of Contrasts

PEOPLE, PLACES, AND EVENTS

Khanbaliq

Kublai Khan

Kublai Khan welcomes Marco Polo

1266
Marco Polo, an explorer from Venice, traveled to China. After meeting him, the Khan sent him on special missions.

Kublai Khan, the leader of Mongolia, **met with explorer Marco Polo**. The Khan became emperor of China in 1271.

Today China's current capital of Beijing is in the same place as the Khan's capital of **Khanbaliq**.

Empress Dowager Cixi

Imperial Palace, Beijing

Rule of an Empress

1898 | The Empress ruled after she forced her nephew, the Emperor, to give up his power.

The **Empress Dowager Cixi** took power in **1898**. She lived at a time of change in China. The rule of emperors and the glory of the **Imperial Palace** was soon to end.

Today you can visit the Imperial Palace in Beijing.

Lesson 1

VOCABULARY

gorge p. 174

steppe p. 177

basin p. 178

READING SKILL

Compare and Contrast
Use the chart below to show how different parts of China have land that is alike and different.

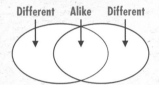

Different   Alike   Different

New York Academic Content Standards

3.1, 3.2, 4.1

The Land of China

People swim near Huangguoshu, the largest waterfall in Asia.

VISUAL PREVIEW

How does the geography of China change from region to region?

A China is large and has many different land regions.

B Eastern China has rivers, coasts, and large cities.

C The north and west have a variety of different land formations.

D Southern and central China have hills, rain forests, and unusual scenery.

A GEOGRAPHY OF CONTRASTS

The third-largest country in the world, China's land changes greatly from area to area. From mountains to coasts, rain forests to deserts—China has everything!

China has all kinds of weather. The climate changes depending on the region you visit. China is divided into twenty-two provinces and has eight main land regions.

QUICK CHECK

Compare and Contrast How is China's division into provinces similar to that of the United States?

Map Skill

PLACE: In what countries is the Gobi Desert?

China: A Land of Many Regions

0 200 400 miles
0 200 400 kilometers

RUSSIA

MONGOLIA

JILIN

INNER MONGOLIA

GOBI

NORTH KOREA

PAKISTAN

Taklimakan Desert

Kunlun Mountains

Beijing ✪

Huang He (Yellow River)

Yellow Sea

JAPAN

TIBET

HIMALAYA

Mt. Everest

CHINA

Shanghai

SICHUAN

Yangtze River

Chang Jiang

Yun Ling Mountains

East China Sea

INDIA

Taipei

Taiwan

YUNNAN

Macau

Hong Kong

PACIFIC OCEAN

VIETNAM

South

International boundary
Provincial boundary

Bay of

Ⓑ EAST COAST

China's east coast is an area of farmland, cities, and waterways. The eastern provinces are known for their silk farms. Many mulberry trees cover the land. Their leaves are the silkworm's favorite food.

Cities and Islands

Along the coast, fishing villages and trading ports have grown into modern cities. The largest is Shanghai, with its skyscrapers and shopping malls. Farther inland, you can see China's capital city of Beijing. Off the eastern coast is the largest island, Taiwan. More islands—Hong Kong, Macau, and tropical Hainan—are found further south.

Rivers

Two great rivers—the Huang He and the Yangtze—meet the China Sea in the east. The mighty Yangtze is the fourth-longest river in the world! It flows through **gorges**, narrow valleys with steep walls. If you follow it inland, you will find many plains that often get flooded. These flat, wet areas, or "floodplains," are perfect for growing rice and farming.

▲ One of the tallest buildings in the world is found in Taipei, Taiwan.

▼ A boat travels through one of the Three Gorges of the Yangtze River.

Where do People Live?

China has a lot of land. However, most of its people live in its eastern provinces. This part of China has the most cities. It also has the best farmland.

QUICK CHECK

Compare and Contrast Why would people want to live in China's eastern provinces instead of the other areas of China?

DataGraphic

World's Largest Countries and Their Populations, 2004

Study the table and map below. Answer the questions that follow.

Population, 2004

Country	Population
Russia	143,202,000
Canada	32,268,000
China	1,315,844,000
United States	298,213,000
Brazil	186,405,000

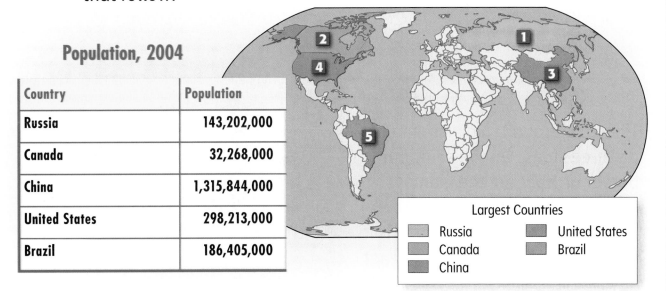

Largest Countries
- Russia
- Canada
- China
- United States
- Brazil

Think About Land Size and Population

1. Which country is larger in terms of land, the United States or Russia?

2. Which country had the largest population in the world in 2004?

LANDS TO THE WEST AND NORTH

China's land climbs high into the mountains in the west. As you move north, you will find dry deserts and grassy plains.

The Tibetan Highlands

Much of Tibet is a plateau covered by grasslands. There yaks graze. These animals provide milk, butter, meat, and wool.

"Roof of the World"

Tibet is surrounded by mountains on three sides. On the southern border of Tibet are the giant Himalaya mountain ranges. There, Mt. Everest touches the sky. It is the tallest mountain on the planet.

Mount Everest

In northern China, you will find Inner Mongolia. The Mongolian people raise horses and herd sheep and goats on the plains. Today, some herders ride motorcycles to round up their animals!

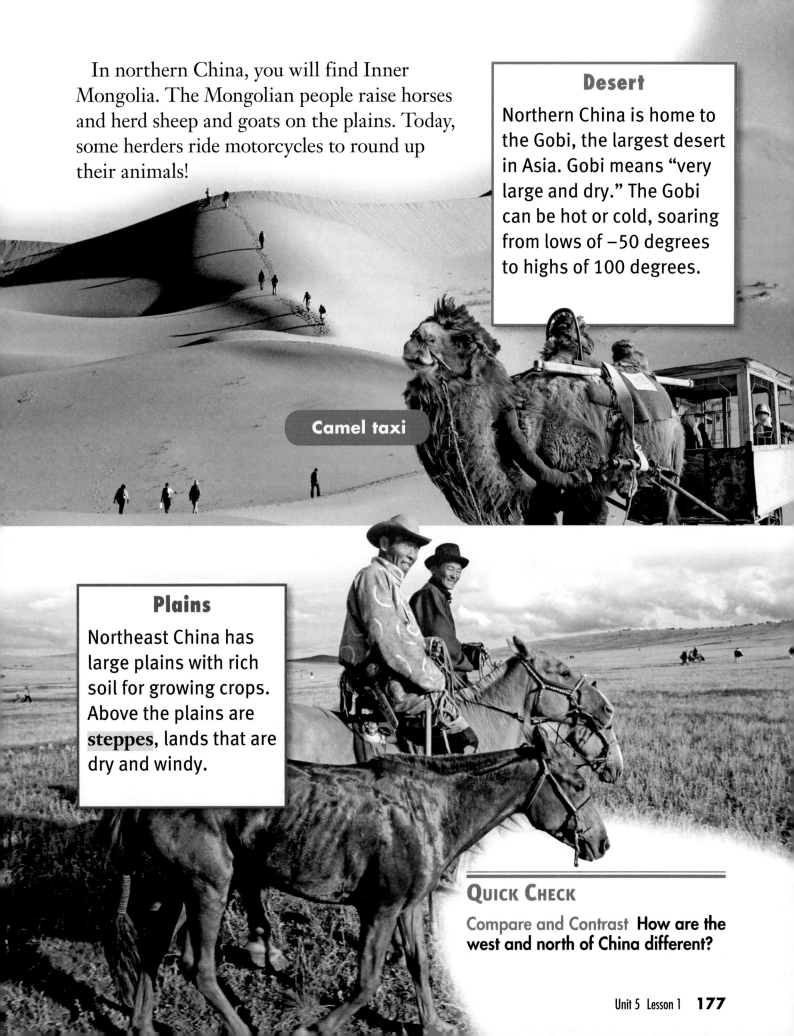

Camel taxi

Desert

Northern China is home to the Gobi, the largest desert in Asia. Gobi means "very large and dry." The Gobi can be hot or cold, soaring from lows of −50 degrees to highs of 100 degrees.

Plains

Northeast China has large plains with rich soil for growing crops. Above the plains are **steppes**, lands that are dry and windy.

QUICK CHECK

Compare and Contrast **How are the west and north of China different?**

Ⓓ CENTRAL AND SOUTHERN LAND

China's central land is a productive area for agriculture. Its hills and valleys and mild climate are good for growing crops.

The Sichuan Basin

In south-central China is an area called the Sichuan Basin. This **basin**, a round lowland, is protected from the wind. So much of China's rice is grown here that it is often called "China's Rice Bowl." Many other crops grow in the Sichuan Basin, such as wheat and cotton.

▲ Rare golden monkeys live in the cloud forests of the Yunling Mountains in the south.

PLACES

In the heart of China is the Wolong Panda Reserve. At Wolong, in the Sichuan Province, pandas are rescued and bred. Some are released into the wild. The giant panda lives best in mountain forests where it can find its main food, bamboo.

Wolong Panda Reserve

Rice is grown on terraced paddies, fields built on a hillside that are flooded.

Karst peaks can be seen
from the Li River.

Karst in the South

If you travel south to the
province of Yunnan, you will see
some of China's most unusual
scenery. In the Stone Forest are
many large stones of different
shapes. This is known as karst
landscape. Karst is a landscape in
which water has worn away the
rocks over time so that they have
strange and beautiful forms.

QUICK CHECK

Compare and Contrast **How does
karst differ from other hills?**

Check Understanding

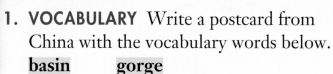

1. **VOCABULARY** Write a postcard from
   China with the vocabulary words below.
   basin   **gorge**

2. **READING SKILL Compare
   and Contrast** Use your chart
   from page 172 to write a
   paragraph about similar and
   different types of land in China.

Different   Alike   Different

3. **Write About It** How
   does China's land change as you
   move west to east?

Map and Globe Skills

Use Map Scales

VOCABULARY

map scale

A map is always much smaller than the place it shows. A map uses a **map scale** to show the real distances between two places. For example, one inch on a map scale can stand for 500 miles. The map scale has marks that stand for the distances.

Learn It

- Read the title of the map on page 181. This map shows China and some of its cities, mountains, and rivers.

- Look at the map scale. The line is two inches long. The map scale shows that two inches on the map equals 1,000 miles on Earth. Copy the mile marks and numbers of the map scale onto the edge of a piece of paper.

- Find Beijing on the map. Place your map scale on Beijing so that the 0 mark is on the dot for Beijing. Move the edge of the paper so that the 600-mile mark is on the dot for Shanghai. The distance from Beijing to Shanghai is about 600 miles.

Shanghai's skyline shows many modern buildings.

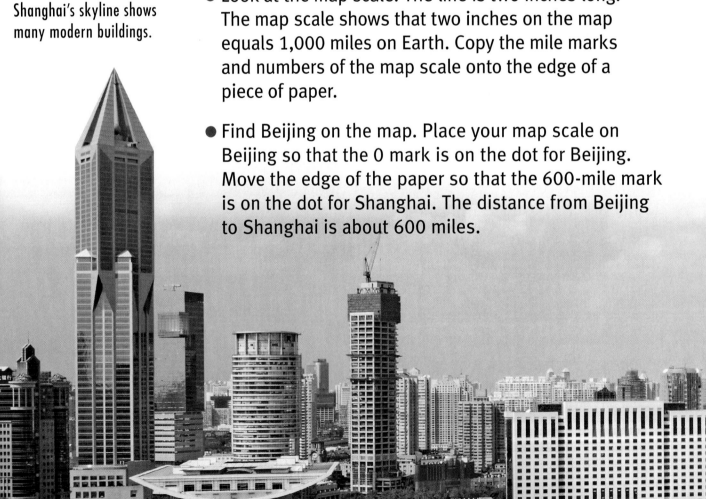

Try It

Using your scale, measure distances on the map below.

- Is the distance from Shanghai to Hong Kong more or less than 1,000 miles?

- Is it more or less than 1,000 miles from Hong Kong to Taipei in Taiwan?

Apply It

- How would you use the scale to measure 2,000 miles on the map?

- About how far is it from the western city of Kashi to the eastern city of Shanghai?

- About how far is it from Hainan Island in the south to the town of Mohe in the northeast?

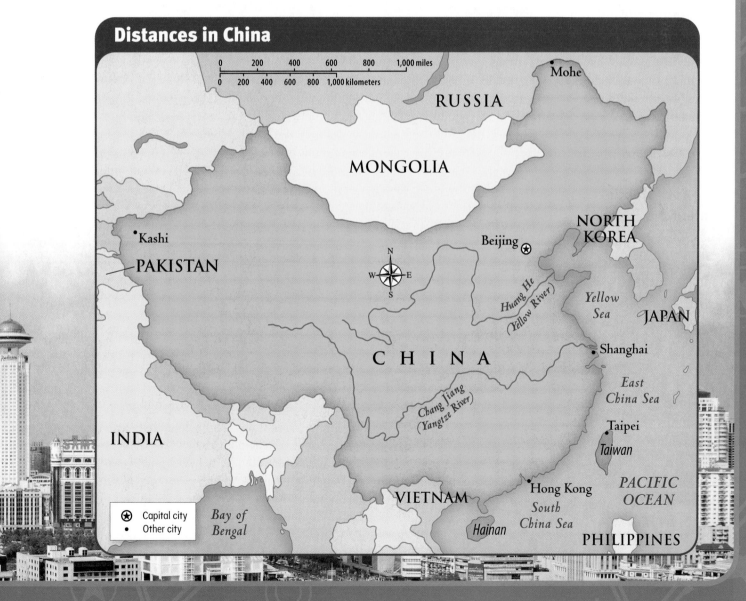

Distances in China

VOCABULARY

dynasty p. 183

porcelain p. 184

compass p. 184

rebel p. 186

imperial p. 186

READING SKILL

Compare and Contrast
Use the chart below to list similarities and differences in the groups that have controlled China.

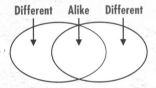

Different   Alike   Different

New York Academic Content Standards

2.1, 2.2, 2.3, 2.4, 5.1

The History of China

An army made of clay soldiers was buried near the tomb of Emperor Qin. They were meant to protect him.

VISUAL PREVIEW

How has leadership and control within China changed?

A Different groups ruled different parts of China until the land was united.

B Chinese emperors built a Great Wall to keep out northern invaders.

C In the 1900s, Chinese rebel groups ended the rule of emperors.

A   EMPERORS AND INVADERS

Archaeologists found the skull of a prehistoric man on a hill near Beijing. He may have lived as much as half a million years ago! This is a clue to China's long history.

Chinese culture owes its beginnings to ancient peoples. They became farmers who built houses and made metal tools. Over time, they built cities and were the first people known to develop writing.

The Chinese Empire

For thousands of years, **dynasties,** or ruling families, controlled China. However, China was made up of smaller states who often fought each other. An empire that united the land was first set up in 221 B.C. by the Qin dynasty. Chinese rulers became known as emperors. The Chinese empire, ruled by dynasties, lasted until the 1900s. Even invaders such as the Mongol leader Kublai Khan could not control China for long.

The grand palaces of the emperors had beautiful gardens. ▼

QUICK CHECK

Compare and Contrast
How did China change in 221 B.C.?

PEOPLE

Qin Shihuangdi was the first Qin emperor. He ordered the connecting of defensive walls that would become the Great Wall.

Qin Shihuangdi

Can you think of things invented in China? **Porcelain**, the **compass**, paper, and kites are all found around the world. Porcelain is fine, thin pottery made from white clay. A compass is an instrument for showing directions. All these items first came from China.

A Project of Length

The Great Wall is China's most amazing invention. It is located in the north of China and was meant to protect the Chinese empire from northern invaders.

▲ Porcelain vases such as this were invented in ancient China.

▼ This compass from the time of the Ming Dynasty also has a sundial.

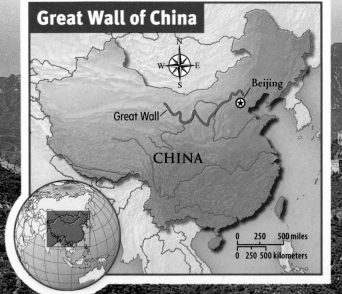

Great Wall of China

N
W · E
S

Beijing

Great Wall

CHINA

0   250   500 miles
0 250 500 kilometers

▶ Paper in China was first made from bamboo fibers.

It was not built by one single emperor. Instead, many rulers added to it over hundreds of years. In the beginning, it was made from earth and stones. Later, bricks and blocks were used. It took thousands of workers to construct it. Today, the wall is about 1,500 miles long!

QUICK CHECK

Compare and Contrast How did the way in which the Great Wall was built change over the years?

Kites have been flown in China for over two thousand years. ▶

The Great Wall we see today was mostly built during the Ming Dynasty, between 1300 and 1600.

C A TIME OF CHANGE

In the 1800s, many Chinese people felt that the emperors were not doing what was best for the country. They tried to make changes. By the mid-1900s, China had become a very different country.

A Fight for A Better Life

In 1851 many Chinese from a group called the Taipings **rebelled,** or fought back, against the Qing Dynasty. They said that it was too cruel and backward. But the Taiping Rebellion did not go well. By 1864 millions of people had died in the fighting. The rebellion was put down by the Qing.

The Empire Weakens

Other countries were trading with China, and some wanted more control. The old **imperial** system, one of emperor rule, was losing power. By 1912 Pu Yi, the emperor, was forced by rebels to give up the throne.

▲ In 1908 Pu Yi became the emperor of China. He was only two years old.

EVENT

In 1842 Great Britain won a war with China and took control of Hong Kong. Hong Kong became an important trading port for the British. By the late 1900s, the colony's economy had become very successful. In 1997 Britain returned Hong Kong to China.

Britain Rules Hong Kong

▶ In 1949 the Communist army entered Beijing and took over the capital.

Revolution

More rebellions took place in the early 1900s. Then, in 1911, a revolution ended dynasty rule. A national state with a president was set up in 1912 by the Nationalists. This state did not last for a long time, however. Another group, the Communists, wanted a workers' state. They fought the Nationalists in a civil war. Finally, in 1949, the Communists won control and renamed China the People's Republic of China. The Nationalists escaped to Taiwan and set up a government there.

QUICK CHECK

Compare and Contrast How was the 1851 rebellion similar to and different from the 1911 revolution?

Check Understanding

1. **VOCABULARY** Use the vocabulary words below to write a sentence about China's emperors.
   dynasty   **imperial**

2. **READING SKILL Compare and Contrast** Use the chart on page 182 to write a paragraph about how control changed in China over the years.

3. **Write About It** How did imperial rule affect China's history?

Lesson 3

VOCABULARY

communism p. 189

political party p. 189

READING SKILL

Compare and Contrast
Use the chart below to write about how a communist system is different from democracy.

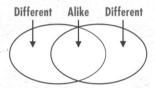

Different   Alike   Different

New York Academic Content Standards
2.1, 2.2, 2.3, 2.4, 5.1, 5.2, 5.4

Governing CHINA

China's government meets in the Great Hall of the People in Beijing.

VISUAL PREVIEW

How does the government work within China?

A Communism is very different from democracy.

B Education first focused on communism, but now teaches many subjects.

Ⓐ NEW RULES

The Chinese people fought hard for a new government. The Communists won. How has life changed in China under Communist rule?

What is **communism**? It is a system in which property and goods are owned by the government and are to be shared equally by everyone.

Communism in China

The People's Republic of China is ruled by the Communist Party. A **political party** is a group that directs government. The chart below shows you some differences between communism and democracy, the system of government in the United States.

▲ The large star on China's flag stands for the Communist Party, and the smaller stars stand for workers.

Two Kinds of Government

Communism	Democracy
One political party	More than one political party
No free elections	Individuals elect representatives to govern
The community owns all goods and the means of production	Individuals can own businesses and freely trade goods for profit
Headed by a central committee and a chairman	Headed by a congress and a president

QUICK CHECK

Compare and Contrast **What is similar between communism and democracy?**

EDUCATING THE PEOPLE

Chinese culture has always seen learning as important. Confucius, one of the most famous Chinese scholars, taught that you could improve yourself through study. What do you think is important to learn?

Learning About Communism

When the Communists first came to power in the 1950s and 1960s, they worked hard to convince people that communism was the best system of government. That kind of teaching was called re-education. It was for adults as well as for children. Everyone was also taught to follow the Communist leader Mao Zedong.

Student Life

During this time, many college students joined an organization called the Red Guard to support for the Communist Party. Colleges were closed, and education in general was disorganized. By the 1970s, Chinese students lagged behind the rest of the world in many subjects.

▲ During imperial times, a test was given to anyone who wanted to work for the government.

In China under Mao, students would often read from The Little Red Book, a collection of his writings. ▶

◀ In China, more girls attend school today than in earlier times.

Chinese Education Today

Education has changed in China. In 1986 the Chinese government passed a law saying children must go to school for at least nine years. At first, the most important subjects were Chinese and math. Now students also learn other subjects, such as science, history, and the arts.

People in China feel the government does not give schools enough money. School for the first nine years is free, but parents must pay for books, food, transportation, and sometimes heat. Many families cannot afford to send their children to college. People see room for more improvements.

QUICK CHECK

Compare and Contrast How has education changed in China since the 1950s and 1960s?

Check Understanding

1. **VOCABULARY** Use the vocabulary words below to write a sentence about the government of China under Mao.
   communism   **political party**

2. **READING SKILL Compare and Contrast** Use your chart from page 188 to write a paragraph about communism and democracy.

Different   Alike   Different

3. **Write About It** Why did the Communists push for reeducation in the 1950s and 1960s?

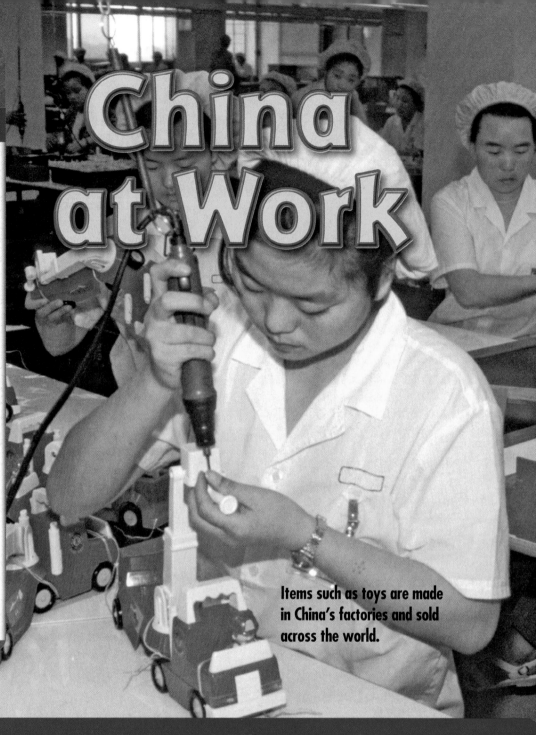

Lesson 4

VOCABULARY

technology p. 193

boom p. 196

dam p. 196

deforestation p. 196

READING SKILL

Compare and Contrast
Use the chart below to write about the things that have helped China's economy grow in the past and present.

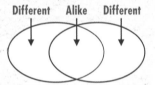

Different   Alike   Different

New York Academic Content Standards
3.1, 3.2, 4.1, 4.2

China at Work

Items such as toys are made in China's factories and sold across the world.

VISUAL PREVIEW How does China's economy connect it with different parts of the world?

A Routes across Asia helped China bring its goods to other countries.

B China's different regions produce different goods to sell at home or abroad.

C Today, China's economy is growing both locally and globally.

Ⓐ A LAND OF RICHES

For thousands of years, people traveled along land and sea routes to reach China and bring home its silk, tea, spices, and fine porcelain.

As people traveled, they also exchanged ideas such as **technology**, the knowledge and skills to make new things.

Ginger, a Chinese spice, is dried, pickled, and candied. ▼

Trade and Travel

Long ago a series of routes called the Silk Road allowed China to trade with Europe and Asia. In eastern China, a giant waterway, the Grand Canal, was built to make shipping easier.

QUICK CHECK

Compare and Contrast **How might the Silk Road have improved trade?**

Dried star anise is a spice from China that is still exported to other countries. ▼

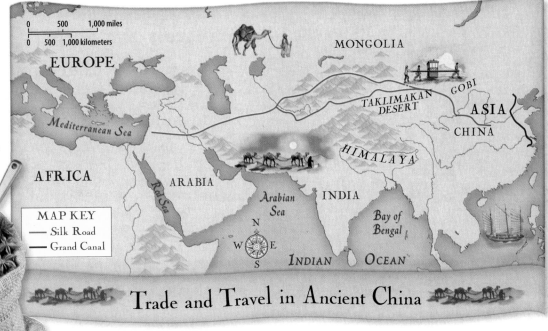

MAP KEY
— Silk Road
— Grand Canal

Trade and Travel in Ancient China

Making Silk Clothing

1. The leaves of mulberry trees are fed to silkworms.

2. The silkworm creates a cocoon by spinning silk thread around itself.

B USING CHINA'S RESOURCES

Today, China's economy owes a lot to its plentiful natural resources. China uses its natural resources to make many products to export around the world. What products are made in China today?

Minerals and Herbs

China has the largest reserves of coal in the world. In the western parts of China, many minerals are mined from the ground. The country's forests and open spaces are home to a wide variety of plants and wildlife. Many medicinal herbs come from southeastern forests.

◀ Tea is made from the leaves of teabushes.

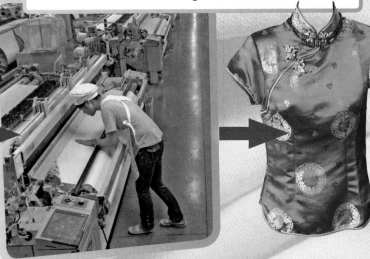

3. A yarn is made from the silk threads in the cocoons.

4. The yarn is woven into silk cloth. The cloth is used to make clothing, such as this shirt.

Rice, Silk, and Electronics

Rich land in the east has made China's rice harvest the largest in the world. The east is also home to many silk farms. With its long coastline, China is the world's top fishing nation. Its coastal waters provide seafood for the country's large population. China's eastern cities make goods like toys, shoes, computers, and other electronics.

QUICK CHECK

Compare and Contrast **How do products and resources in the east of China differ from those in the west?**

Fishermen sell their catch in a Chinese port. ▶

Ⓑ MODERN CHANGES

▲ The word "yuan" means round coin. The Chinese yuan used to be a silver coin.

China's economy has improved greatly in the last 25 to 30 years. There has been a **boom,** a time of quick growth, in China's industries. Now China has one of the strongest economies in the world.

Business Grows

In 1979 other countries were invited to do business with China. New companies and factories started to open in China. With them came new machines, money, and other technology. In 1999 China signed a trade agreement with the United States. In 2001 China joined a group called the World Trade Organization.

Signs of Improvement

Transportation in China has improved greatly. There are now better railroads. Tourism, or the business of hosting visitors, has also grown into a major business. The yuan, China's money, is much stronger than in past decades. Most people in the cities make a better living than they did 30 years ago.

Water Power

Giant **dams** on the major rivers make China one of the world's largest producers of hydropower, or power produced by water. A dam is a wall or structure built across a river to hold back and control the water.

Citizenship

Joining a Citizen's Group

In the past fifteen years, many Chinese citizens have created their own groups to improve their communities. One issue that people want to improve is caring for the environment. Groups must register and receive approval from their local government. Some of the issues that groups work to improve are pollution, garbage disposal, and deforestation. **Deforestation** is the destruction of forests.

Write About It On what other projects could citizen's groups work?

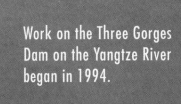

Work on the Three Gorges Dam on the Yangtze River began in 1994.

Growth Brings Problems

Growth can bring problems. Thousands of people are moving from farms to cities, making the cities crowded. A boom in industry means more power is needed to run factories, cars, and homes. This can cause pollution in the environment. As its population and economy continue to grow, China will have to find new ways to prevent or fix these problems.

QUICK CHECK

Summarize What are some reasons that China's economy has grown in the last 30 years?

Check Understanding

1. **VOCABULARY** Use these vocabulary words in two sentences to tell how China uses resources.
   boom   **technology**

2. **READING SKILL Compare and Contrast** Use your chart from page 192 to write a paragraph about what has helped China's economy grow.

3. **Write About It** How has global trade affected China?

Lesson 5

VOCABULARY

architecture p. 200

pagoda p. 200

courtyard p. 202

cooperate p. 203

READING SKILL

Compare and Contrast
As you read, think about ancient Chinese arts and customs and ways that China's culture is alive today.

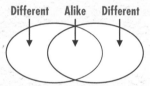

Different   Alike   Different

New York Academic Content Standards
2.1, 2.2, 2.3, 2.4, 3.1

Living in China

These girls are learning kung fu, a kind of fighting practice.

VISUAL PREVIEW

How does life vary in different times and regions of China?

A China celebrates both ancient festivals and modern holidays.

B Traditional arts are practiced at home and influenced by the world.

C Life in rural villages varies based on the land and the climate.

D The city of Beijing is both modern and historic.

A COMMUNITY LIFE

Chinese culture has developed over thousands of years. Many of its oldest traditions are kept alive today, such as the celebrations of the Chinese New Year.

Communities in China come together to celebrate festivals during the year. The Chinese have both ancient festivals and modern holidays. At some, special foods, such as mooncakes or dumplings, are eaten.

Chinese New Year

The most important holiday is the Chinese New Year. It falls in January or February every year and lasts for 15 days. Families enjoy a large feast together. They make wishes and prayers, and honor those who have died. Fireworks are set off, and everyone wears red.

Dragon-shaped lanterns decorate a park for the Longsha Lantern Festival. ▲

QUICK CHECK

Compare and Contrast **How is China's culture both ancient and modern?**

Children perform dances in a New Year celebration. ▼

One part of a culture is its **architecture**, or the style of its buildings. If you travel in China, you will see **pagodas**. Pagodas are old, wooden temples with graceful roofs that curve upwards.

Ancient Crafts

Many of China's arts are traditional because they are based on ancient ways. Each is a special craft that requires special skills, tools, and materials. One example is the art of creating beautifully decorated porcelain, also known as "china." Silk weaving is another art that started in China. At first, the Chinese kept these crafts a secret. Today they are also practiced in other parts of the world.

Living Arts

Have you ever heard Chinese music? It sounds very different from music in other parts of the world. One reason is because it is played on unique Chinese instruments. Today, Chinese music also includes European and American styles and instruments.

▲ The Yellow Crane Pagoda has been rebuilt many times.

▼ Chinese performances come to life through music, dance, and traditional costumes.

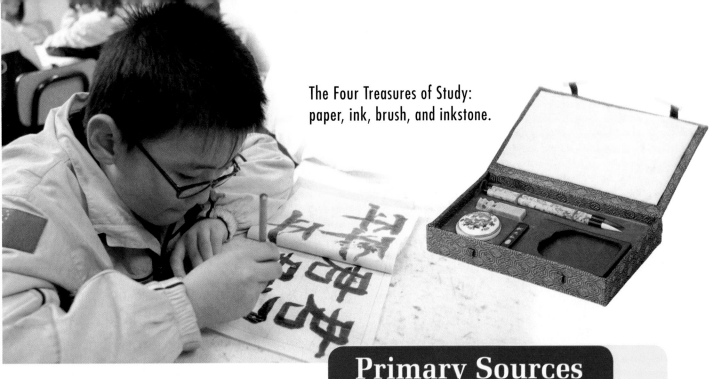

The Four Treasures of Study: paper, ink, brush, and inkstone.

The Art of the Brush

Chinese art and poetry often use nature as a subject, such as China's mountains and rivers. Traditional Chinese art was painted on silk or rice paper and hung as scrolls. It often included poems. Chinese calligraphy, which means "beautiful writing," also is considered an art. The same type of brush and ink is used for both painting and calligraphy.

Writing has been a part of China's culture for a long time. The ideas of the Chinese thinker Confucius were written down and taught across China. People still quote his sayings.

QUICK CHECK

Compare and Contrast How has Chinese music changed?

Primary Sources

The Golden Rule

One of the most well-known quotations from Confucius is the idea of the "golden rule," which states:

"What you do not want done to yourself, do not do to others."

Teachings from Confucius (551–479 B.C.)

Write About It Have you heard these teachings before? Write a paragraph explaining in your own words one of Confucius' teachings.

C   RURAL LIFE

China has some of the largest cities in the world. Many people live in the crowded, busy cities. Still, village life continues. What is life like in the countryside of China?

Living in A Village

Three out of four people in China live in small towns or farming villages. People still get around by bicycle, by by boat, or by foot. Most village homes are not modern, but some have electricity. Almost every village home has a **courtyard**, an open area surrounded by buildings. This is the center of daily life. Here people do their washing, sewing, and cooking. Family life is important, and many generations may live together.

▲ This woman drives to the village market.

People Adapt

The people in China have learned to adapt their lives to the land's features and climate. Their houses and farms look different depending on the area of China you are visiting. In Inner Mongolia, people called Mongols live on grasslands in round tents called yurts.

Houses line this canal in eastern China. ▼

Yurts are covered with hides and can be moved easily. ▼

▲ People ride bicycles past apartments in the small town of Nanjie, home of the largest instant noodle company in the world.

A Joint Effort

Everyone in a farming village works hard and **cooperates**, or helps each other, to bring in crops. People also share the daily activities that provide for their family. They might help with gardening, making clothes, or fixing tools.

Feeding the Family

Every day, the Chinese people eat 3 billion bowls of rice! Rice, noodles, vegetables, fish, and tofu are common foods used in Chinese cooking. Villagers catch their fish in nearby ponds, streams, or rivers. Their meat comes from chickens, ducks, and pigs found in the town. Some dishes are prepared over a fire in a wok, a big round pan.

▲ Steamed buns made from wheat are a popular food item in China.

QUICK CHECK

Compare and Contrast **How is living in a Chinese village different from the way you live?**

A CITY FOR ALL TIMES

Beijing has been China's capital on and off over the last two thousand years. Today you can see both its old and new sides!

A Fast Pace

Beijing's streets are so crowded, you might prefer to take the subway, called the "Underground Dragon"! Even in the 1300s, the capital was a busy scene. Marco Polo, an Italian explorer, wrote that "every day more than 1,000 cartloads of silk enter the city." Today, people are rushing to work in offices or factories.

Experiencing Beijing

You can taste the famous Peking Roast Duck at a restaurant or relax in a teahouse. The Chinese are already preparing their city for a big event. In 2008 the World Summer Olympics will be hosted by China and held in Beijing!

Many people shop in the modern stores of Beijing or in its traditional street markets. ▼

▲ People enter Tiananmen Square by walking through Tiananmen Gate.

Back to the Emperors

You can learn about life during the time of emperors in the Temple of Heaven, the Ming Tombs, and the Summer Palace.

Then visit the Imperial City and walk through Tiananmen Square. At the north end is the historic Forbidden City. The Forbidden City is home to the Imperial Palace, built in the 1400s. Anyone who was not invited to enter by the emperor was "forbidden." At its center is the Hall of Supreme Harmony. Within this hall sits a golden throne that used to seat the Chinese emperor. Although these times are in the past, you can imagine China's rich history.

QUICK CHECK

Compare and Contrast **What makes life in Beijing both old and new?**

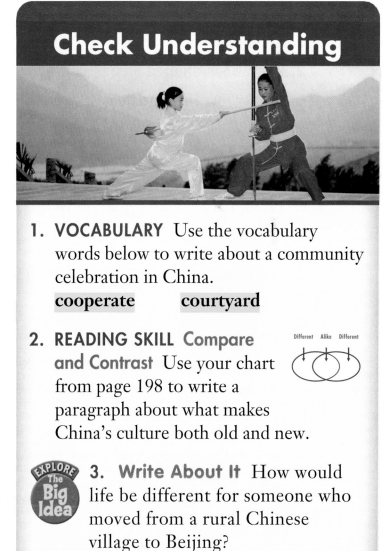

Check Understanding

1. **VOCABULARY** Use the vocabulary words below to write about a community celebration in China.
   cooperate   **courtyard**

2. **READING SKILL Compare and Contrast** Use your chart from page 198 to write a paragraph about what makes China's culture both old and new.

3. **Write About It** How would life be different for someone who moved from a rural Chinese village to Beijing?

Unit 5 Review and Assess

Vocabulary

Number a paper from 1 to 3. Beside each number write the word from the list below that matches the number.

cooperate   **dynasty**   **basin**

1. a ruling family
2. a low, bowl-shaped area of land
3. to work together and help one another

Comprehension and Critical Thinking

4. What happened to imperial rule in China in the 1900s?
5. Why is education in China better today than it was under Mao Zedong?
6. **Reading Skill** How has technology affected China today and in the time of the Silk Road?
7. **Critical Thinking** What are some ways that traditions are continued in China?

Skill

Use Map Scales

Use the scale of miles to measure distances on the map at right. Write a complete sentence to answer each question.

8. How far is it from Tiananmen Square to the Temple of Heaven?
9. How far is it from the Forbidden City to Beihei Park?
10. How wide is the distance between the walls of the Forbidden City?

Beijing

N W E S

Beibai Park

Imperial Palace

FORBIDDEN CITY

□ Park
■ Point of interest

■ TIANANMEN SQUARE

0   0.5   1 mile
0   0.5   1 kilometer

Temple of Heaven Park

New York English Language Arts Test Preparation

Directions

Read this paragraph about food in China. Then answer questions 1 through 3.

You can tell a lot about a country's culture by its food. Chinese people eat rice with almost every meal. This is because rice grows well in the rich land along rivers in the south and the east. Because so many people spend their lives farming, they celebrate the growing seasons with festivals. These almost always include big feasts of favorite Chinese foods—dumplings, noodles, sweet cakes, and . . . rice.

---

1 What is **one** reason that the Chinese eat so much rice?

  A It tastes great.

  B It grows well in China.

  C Rice is expensive.

  D They do not eat rice.

2 According to this paragraph, many people in China are _____.

  A miners

  B lawyers

  C doctors

  D farmers

3 Where in China does rice grow?

  A east and south

  B north and south

  C north and west

  D east and west

Review

How do differences exist within and between communities?

Write About the Big Idea

Descriptive Essay

Think about how China is a country of contrasts—both old and modern. Use your completed Foldable to help you write an essay that answers the Big Idea question, "How do differences exist within and between communities?" Your essay should focus on the ways that China has stayed the same and the ways China has changed through its history. Each idea you write should be supported by details from the lessons. Then write a conclusion.

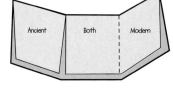

Make a Class Population Poster

Work together in small groups to make a class population poster. Your poster should show the number of students in the class and a map of the places they come from. Here's how to make your population poster.

1. Gather information about a class in your school. Find out how many students are in the class and where they are from.

2. Make a table that lists all the cities or countries that students are from. Write down the number of students that come from each place and the total number of students.

3. Make a map showing all the places students in the class are from.

4. Give your poster a title.

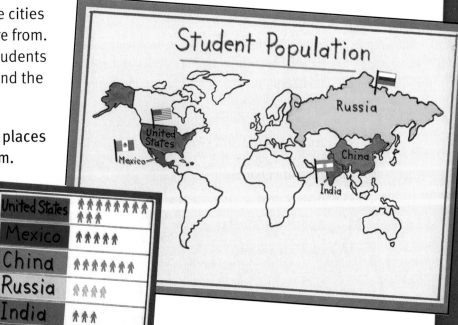

Reference Section

The Reference Section has many parts, each with a different type of information. Use this section to look up people, places, and events as you study.

**Unit 1 Reading Skill:
Main Idea and Details** R2

Unit 2 Reading Skill: Sequence R4

Unit 3 Reading Skill: Summarize R6

Unit 4 Reading Skill: Cause and Effect . . R8

**Unit 5 Reading Skill:
Compare and Contrast** R10

Geography Handbook GH1

Atlas GH12

Glossary REF1

Index REF5

Credits REF11

Main Idea and Details

The **main idea** is what the paragraph is about. It is what the author wants you to understand about the subject. Often the main idea is in the first sentence of a paragraph. The other sentences have **details** that tell more about the main idea. Finding the main idea and details will help you understand what you read.

Learn It

- **Read the paragraph.** Think about what the paragraph is about. See if there is a sentence which states the main idea.

- **Now look for details.** Sentences with details give more information about the main idea.

Main Idea	
The first sentence states the main idea.	Mexico has many natural resources, which are materials found in nature that people use. Examples of natural resources include oil, silver, and crops. People use these resources to make products, such as jewelry and clothing.
Details These details tell some of the resources that Mexico has.	

Try It

Copy and complete the chart. Write the main idea and the details of the paragraph from page R2 in the boxes.

Main Idea	Details

Apply It

● Review the steps in Learn It.

● Read the paragraph below. Then make a main idea and details chart for the paragraph.

The largest park in Mexico City is Chapultepec Park. It includes the former home to Mexican presidents, Chapultepec Castle. You can also see rare native artifacts in the National Museum of Anthropology, located in the park.

Unit 2 • Reading Skills

Sequence

The paragraph below tells about the conflicts England and France had over Canada. When you read, think about the **sequence**, or order, of events. Thinking about the order of events will help you understand and remember what you read.

Learn It

- Look for clue words such as first, next, later, and last. These words can help show the order of events.

- Look for dates that tell exactly when things happened.

First Event
England begins trading in Canada.

Clue words
These words help you recognize other events.

England set up trading centers in Canada in the early 1600s. Both the English and the French were now trading with native Canadians. They both wanted to control trade in Canada. The next step was war. The war ended in 1763. England now controlled most of the land.

Dates
Dates help you keep events in order.

Try It

Copy and complete this chart. Write the events from the paragraph from page R4 in the correct sequence. You may need to add boxes to the chart to show more events.

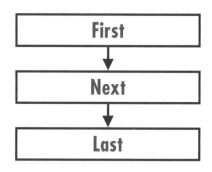

First
↓
Next
↓
Last

Apply It

- Review the sequencing steps in Learn It.

- Read the paragraph below. Then create a sequence of events chart to show the order of events.

On July 1, 1867, the Canadian Confederation was formed. The four original provinces of the Canadian Federation were Quebec, Ontario, Nova Scotia, and New Brunswick. Later, more provinces and territories would join. In 1885 the building of the Canadian-Pacific Railway linked Canada from east to west. By 1905 Alberta and Saskatchewan joined the Confederation.

Unit 3 • Reading Skills
Summarize

How do you tell a friend about a book or movie? You might retell the story in your own words. Of course, you don't tell every single thing that happened. You tell the important parts. To retell a story this way is to summarize. **Summarizing** what you have read can help you remember information in social studies.

Learn It

- Read the whole selection. Try to state what the selection is about in your own words.

- Find important supporting details and combine them.

- Write one or two sentences to summarize what the whole selection is telling you.

Main Idea
This is a main idea. Use it to begin your summary.

Details
These details support the main idea. They can be combined.

Some people say that South Africa has the greatest wildlife show on earth. South Africa's creatures range from A to Z—antelopes to zebras—with many animals in between. Most of South Africa's animals live on game reserves. Animals are protected from hunters on game reserves.

Many people go on safaris. A safari is a trip to an African game reserve. You can here the thunder of elephants marching. In the grass, you might see cheetahs and lions.

Now copy the chart. Fill in the boxes to summarize the paragraphs on page R6.

Write a summary of the selection on page R6.

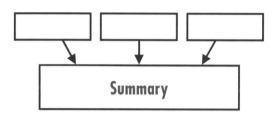

Summary

Apply It

- Review the summarizing steps in Learn It.

- Make a chart like the one above. Use it to summarize the paragraphs below.

In 1948 the government of South Africa started the policy of apartheid. This meant that black people and white people had to live apart. The government divided the land into white and black areas. The whites got most of the land. The blacks had to live in the poorest parts, called homelands.

Black people in South Africa fought hard to have equal rights. Nelson Mandela helped to lead the fight to end apartheid. Apartheid finally fell apart, piece by piece, in the early 1990s.

Cause and Effect

Think about the last time you spent money. You had a reason. A **cause**, or reason, is why something happens. An **effect** is what happens. Thinking about causes and effects will help you understand events you read about.

Learn It

- To find a cause, ask, "Why did it happen?"

- To find an effect, ask, "What happened?"

- Look for words such as because, as a result, and so. These words often link causes and effects.

- Now look for causes and effects in the paragraph.

Cause
This sentence tells why important towns are found on the coast.

Clue words
The words "as a result" and "because of" are clue words. These words often link causes and effects.

Italy has more than 2,000 miles of coastline, which is great for trading by boat. As a result, many important towns have grown along the coast. Ships from all over the world enter these busy ports. The seafaring life has been a part of Italian history for years because of Italy's location.

Effect
This is an effect.

Try It

Copy this cause-and-effect chart. Then complete the chart with causes and effects from the paragraph on page R8.

Cause	→	Effect
	→	
	→	
	→	

Apply It

- Review the steps for understanding cause and effect in Learn It.

- Read the paragraph below. Then make a chart to show the causes and effects from the paragraph.

The Roman people built the city of Rome. The power of Rome grew. Its leaders were strong, and they built large armies. Soldiers were well-trained and brave. As a result, they conquered many lands. Soon, the Romans controlled most of Italy. Powerful generals brought more land under Roman control. These areas became known as the Roman Empire.

Unit 5 • Reading Skills
Compare and Contrast

Compare means to see how things are alike.
Contrast means to see how things are different.
Comparing and contrasting will help you understand
what you read in social studies.

Learn It

- To compare two things, look for how they are alike.

- To contrast two things, look for ways they are
  different.

  Now read the passage below. Think about how
  China's economy is similar and different in different
  parts of the country.

Alike
All regions have
plentiful resources.

All make products
for export.

Different
The west mines
minerals from the
ground.

The southeast
produces herbs from
the forest.

The east makes
other goods.

Today, all regions of China owe a lot to
their plentiful natural resources. All of China
uses its natural resources to make many
products to export around the world. In the
western parts of China, many minerals are
mined from the ground. The country's forests
and open spaces are home to a wide variety
of plants and wildlife. Many medicinal herbs
come from the southeastern forests. Rich land
in the east has made China's rice harvest the
largest in the world. China's eastern cities
also make goods like toys, shoes, computers,
and other electronics.

Try It

Copy the Venn Diagram. Then fill in the left-hand side with details about the western part of China. Fill in the right-hand side with details about the eastern part of China. Fill in the center with ways that both regions are similar economically.

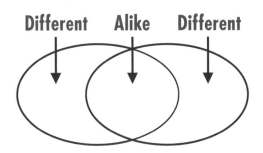

Apply It

- Review the steps for comparing and contrasting in Learn It.

- Read the paragraph below. Then make a Venn Diagram to compare and contrast revolutions in China.

In China, many groups rebelled to change life in their country. In 1911 a revolution ended dynasty rule. A national state with a president was set up in 1912 by the Nationalists. Another group, the Communists, wanted a workers state. They fought the Nationalists in a civil war. They won control of China in 1949.

Geography Handbook

Geography and You GH1

Six Essential Elements GH1

Five Themes of Geography GH2

Dictionary of Geographic Terms .GH4

Reviewing Geography Skills.....GH6

   Looking at Earth GH6

   A Map of the World................GH7

   Reading a Map GH8

   Special Maps: Landform Map......GH10

   Historical Map GH11

Atlas GH12

   United States Political/Physical ...GH12

   World: Political..................GH14

Geography and You

Geography is the study of Earth and the people, plants, and animals that live on it. Most people think of geography as learning about cities, states, and countries, but geography is far more. Geography includes learning about land—mountains, and plains—and bodies of water—oceans, lakes, and rivers.

Geography includes the study of how people adapt to living in a new place. Geography is about how people move around, how they move goods, and how ideas travel from place to place.

Geography includes so many things that geographers have divided this information into six elements, or ideas, so you can better understand them.

Six Essential Elements

The World in Spatial Terms: Where is a place located, and what land or water features does this place have?

Places and Regions: What is special about a place, and what makes it different from another place?

Physical Systems: What has shaped the land and climate of a place, and how does this affect the plants, animals, and people there?

Human Systems: How do people, ideas, and goods move from place to place?

Environment and Society: How have people changed the land and water of a place, and how have the land and water affected the people of a place?

Uses of Geography: How does geography influence events of the past, present, and future?

Five Themes of Geography

You have just read about six essential elements. The five themes of geography are another way to divide the ideas of geography. These themes are location, place, region, movement, and human interaction. They help us think about the world around us. Look for these themes as you read the Map Skill questions throughout the book.

1. Location

The White House

In geography, location means an exact spot on the planet. A location often means a street name and number, such as 1600 Pennsylvania Avenue, the address of the White House. You write a location when you address a letter.

2. Place

Chicago, Illinois

What makes one place different from another? Every place has physical and human features, such as mountains or lakes, that describe it. Place also includes human features, such as where people live, how they work, and what languages they speak.

3. Region

The Arizona desert

A region is a larger area than a place or location. A region is an area with common features that set it apart from other areas. One region may have many mountains or be mostly desert. People in a region may share customs and language.

4. Movement

Throughout history people have moved things and themselves from one place to another. Geographers study why these movements happen. They also look at how people's movement changes an area.

5. Human Interaction

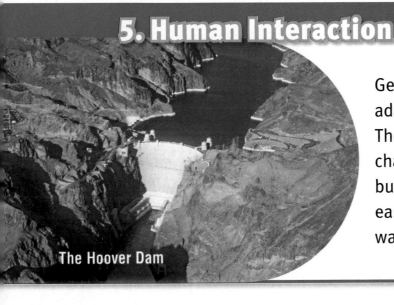

The Hoover Dam

Geographers study how people adapt to their environment. They also study how people change their environment. They build bridges to make travel easier, or build dams to store water and make electricity.

Dictionary of Geographic Terms

1 **BAY** Body of water partly surrounded by land

2 **BEACH** Land covered with sand or pebbles next to an ocean or lake

3 **CANAL** Waterway dug across the land to connect two bodies of water

4 **CANYON** Deep river valley with steep sides

5 **CLIFF** High steep face of rock

6 **COAST** Land next to an ocean

7 **DESERT** A dry environment with few plants and animals

8 **GULF** Body of water partly surrounded by land; larger than a bay

9 **HARBOR** Protected place by an ocean or river where ships can safely stay

10 **HILL** Rounded, raised landform; not as high as a mountain

11 **ISLAND** Land that is surrounded on all sides by water

12 **LAKE** Body of water completely surrounded by land

13 **MESA** Landform that looks like a high, flat table

14 **MOUNTAIN** High landform with steep sides; higher than a hill

15 **OCEAN** Large body of salt water

16 **PENINSULA** Land that has water on all sides but one

17 **PLAIN** Large area of flat land

18 **PLATEAU** High flat area that rises steeply above the surrounding land

19 **PORT** Place where ships load and unload goods

20 **RIVER** Long stream of water that empties into another body of water

21 **VALLEY** Area of low land between hills or mountains

Reviewing Geography Skills

Looking at Earth

Earth and the Globe

From outer space, Earth looks like a big blue ball with green and brown areas of land and white clouds. A globe is a model of Earth. It shows what the land and water look like on Earth.

You can see a line around the widest part of the globe. This is the equator. The equator is an imaginary line that separates the north from the south.

The farthest point north on the globe is called the North Pole. The farthest point south on the globe is called the South Pole.

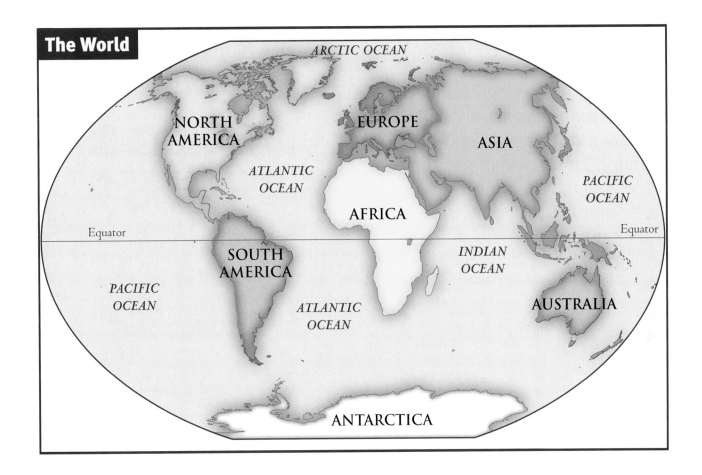

The World

ARCTIC OCEAN

NORTH AMERICA

EUROPE

ASIA

ATLANTIC OCEAN

PACIFIC OCEAN

AFRICA

Equator

Equator

SOUTH AMERICA

INDIAN OCEAN

PACIFIC OCEAN

ATLANTIC OCEAN

AUSTRALIA

ANTARCTICA

A Map of the World

A world map is a flat drawing of Earth. This map shows the continents and the oceans. Unlike a globe, a flat map can be used in a book.

The big areas of land on the Earth are called continents. The big bodies of water are called oceans.

There are seven continents on Earth. There are four major oceans. The equator divides the Earth into the northern half and the southern half.

What are the seven continents of the world?

What are the four oceans?

Reading a Map

A map is a drawing of a place. Some maps show only part of the world. This map shows the United States. Most maps have features that help us read and use maps. Some map features are called out here.

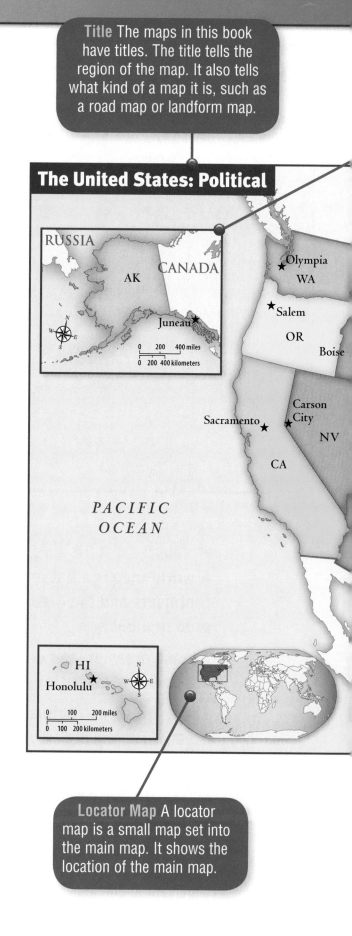

Title The maps in this book have titles. The title tells the region of the map. It also tells what kind of a map it is, such as a road map or landform map.

The United States: Political

RUSSIA

CANADA

AK

Juneau

0 200 400 miles
0 200 400 kilometers

Olympia
WA

Salem

OR

Boise

Carson City

Sacramento

NV

CA

PACIFIC OCEAN

HI
Honolulu

0 100 200 miles
0 100 200 kilometers

Locator Map A locator map is a small map set into the main map. It shows the location of the main map.

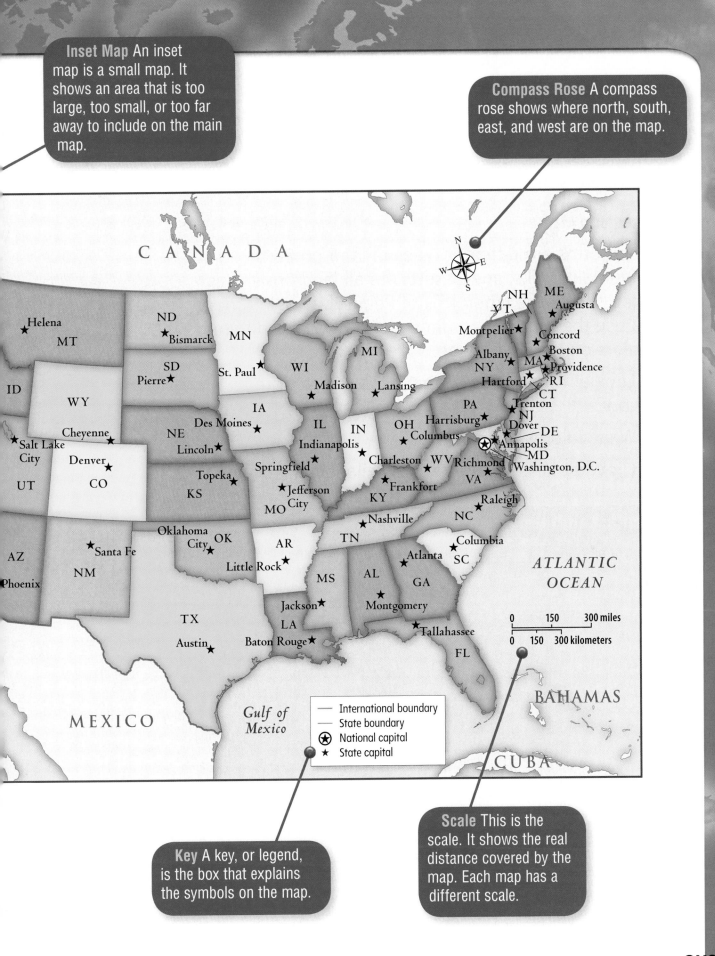

Inset Map An inset map is a small map. It shows an area that is too large, too small, or too far away to include on the main map.

Compass Rose A compass rose shows where north, south, east, and west are on the map.

Key A key, or legend, is the box that explains the symbols on the map.

Scale This is the scale. It shows the real distance covered by the map. Each map has a different scale.

CANADA

Helena
MT
ND
Bismarck
MN
MI
NH ME
Augusta
VT
Montpelier Concord
Boston
SD St. Paul WI Albany MA
Pierre Madison Lansing NY Providence
ID Hartford RI
WY IA CT
Des Moines Trenton
Cheyenne NE IL IN PA NJ
Salt Lake Lincoln Indianapolis OH Harrisburg Dover DE
City Denver Springfield Columbus Annapolis
UT CO Charleston WV Richmond MD
Topeka Jefferson Washington, D.C.
KS City KY Frankfort VA
MO Nashville Raleigh
Oklahoma TN NC
City OK AR Columbia
AZ Santa Fe Little Rock Atlanta SC
NM MS AL GA
Phoenix Jackson Montgomery
TX LA Tallahassee
Austin Baton Rouge FL

St. Paul
WI

ATLANTIC
OCEAN

0   150   300 miles
0   150   300 kilometers

MEXICO
Gulf of
Mexico

BAHAMAS

International boundary
State boundary
National capital
State capital

CUBA

Special Maps

Maps can show many different kinds of information. Here are some kinds of special maps.

Landform Map

Landforms are different types of land on Earth. Mountains, hills, and deserts are all landforms. This map shows the landforms of Pennsylvania. You need to use the map key to understand what the different colors on the map mean.

• Look at the map key. What does the color red show?

• What color is used for hills?

• On what kind of landform is Philadelphia located?

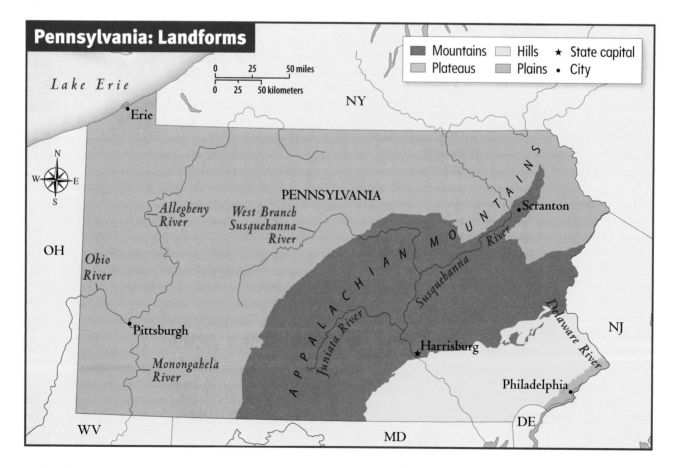

Pennsylvania: Landforms

Key: Mountains, Plateaus, Hills, Plains, ★ State capital, • City

Lake Erie

NY

Erie

PENNSYLVANIA

Allegheny River

West Branch Susquehanna River

OH

Ohio River

Pittsburgh

Monongahela River

APPALACHIAN MOUNTAINS

Juniata River

Susquehanna River

Scranton

Harrisburg

Delaware River

NJ

Philadelphia

WV

MD

DE

0 25 50 miles
0 25 50 kilometers

Historical Maps

A historical map shows how a place appeared at a certain time in the past. Use the key to understand symbols and colors on the map. The key gives details about the time in history. This map shows how our country looked when people from Europe first moved here. It shows the first thirteen colonies.

• What colonies were called the southern colonies?

• What city was a Pilgrim settlement?

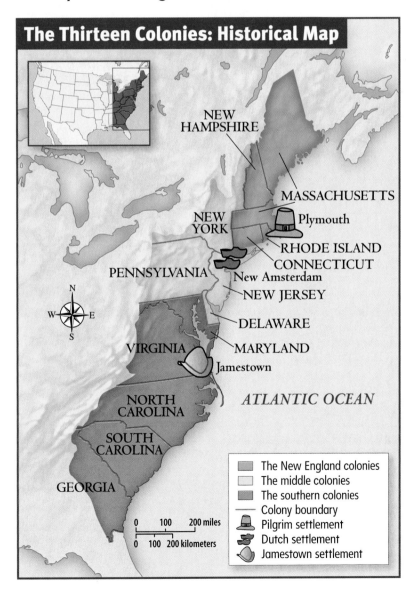

The Thirteen Colonies: Historical Map

NEW HAMPSHIRE

MASSACHUSETTS

NEW YORK

Plymouth

RHODE ISLAND

CONNECTICUT

PENNSYLVANIA

New Amsterdam

NEW JERSEY

DELAWARE

VIRGINIA

MARYLAND

Jamestown

NORTH CAROLINA

ATLANTIC OCEAN

SOUTH CAROLINA

GEORGIA

N W E S

0 100 200 miles
0 100 200 kilometers

- The New England colonies
- The middle colonies
- The southern colonies
— Colony boundary
- Pilgrim settlement
- Dutch settlement
- Jamestown settlement

United States: Political/Physical

ARCTIC OCEAN
70°N

RUSSIA

BROOKS RANGE
ALASKA

Bering Strait

Arctic Circle

60°N

CANADA

Mt. McKinley
20,320 ft.
(6,194 m)

ALASKA RANGE

Yukon River

Bering Sea

Gulf of Alaska

N
W E
S

Aleutian Islands

| 0 | 200 | 400 miles |
| 0 | 200 | 400 kilometers |

170°W   160°W   150°W   140°W

130°W

40°N

PACIFIC OCEAN

Cape Mendocino

San Francisco Bay

Puget Sound
Mt. Rainier
14,410 ft. (4,392 m)   WA

Mt. St. Helens
8,363 ft. (2,549 m)

Columbia R.

Mt. Hood
11,239 ft.
(3,426 m)

CASCADE RANGE

OR

Mt. Shasta
14,162 ft.
(4,317 m)

COAST RANGES

SIERRA NEVADA

Sacramento R.

San Joaquin R.

CENTRAL VALLEY

Lake Tahoe

Mt. Whitney
14,494 ft.
(4,418 m)

Death Valley
-282 ft.
(-86 m)

CA

MOJAVE DESERT

Salton Sea

Channel Islands

COLUMBIA PLATEAU

Snake River

ID

ROCKY

Missouri River

MT

Granite Peak
12,799 ft.
(3,901 m)

WY

BLACK HILLS

Great Salt Lake

GREAT BASIN

GREAT SALT LAKE DESERT

WASATCH RANGE

Kings Peak
13,528 ft.
(4,123 m)

Mt. Elbert
14,433 ft.
(4,399 m)

CO

NV

UT

COLORADO

PLATEAU

Lake Mead

Colorado River

AZ

Humphreys Peak
12,633 ft.
(3,851 m)

Gila River

SONORAN DESERT

M O U N T A I N S

CONTINENTAL DIVIDE

Pikes Peak
14,110 ft. (4,...

Wheeler Peak
13,161 ft.
(4,011 m)

Pecos River

NM

Guadalupe Peak
8,749 ft.
(2,667 m)

Rio Grande

PACIFIC OCEAN

30°N

	Interational boundary
	State boundary
⊛	National capital
▲	Mountain peak
▲	Highest point
▼	Lowest point

160°W   155°W

Kauai   HAWAII

Oahu   N
W E
S

Niihau

Molokai

PACIFIC OCEAN

Lanai   Maui
Kahoolawe

Hawaii

20°N

Mauna Kea
13,796 ft.
(4,205 m)

| 0 | 100 | 200 miles |
| 0 | 100 | 200 kilometers |

Gulf of California

MEXICO

| 0 | 200 | 400 miles |
| 0 | 200 | 400 kilometers |

Tropic of Cancer

20°N

120°W   110°W

GH12

CANADA

Lake of the Woods

MESABI RANGE

Lake Superior

GREAT LAKES

St. Lawrence River

ME

ND

MN

Lake Huron

Lake Ontario

Mt. Washington 6,288 ft. (1,917 m)

VT

GREEN MOUNTAINS

NH

ADIRONDACK MOUNTAINS

Cape Cod

Mississippi River

WI

Lake Michigan

MI

Hudson River

MA

SD

NY

Lake Erie

CT

RI

40°N

GREAT PLAINS

ALLEGHENY PLATEAU

APPALACHIAN MOUNTAINS

Susquehanna River

Long Island

NE

CENTRAL PLAINS

IA

River

OH

ALLEGHENY MOUNTAINS

PA

NJ

Missouri River

IL

IN

River

WV

MD DE

Washington, D.C.

Delaware Bay

Platte River

Potomac River

KS

Wabash River

Ohio River

VA

Chesapeake Bay

MO

PIEDMONT

m)

INTERIOR PLAINS

OZARK PLATEAU

KY

Mt. Mitchell 6,684 ft. (2,037 m)

NC

Cape Hatteras

Arkansas River

TN

Tennessee River

OK

OUACHITA MOUNTAINS

AR

SC

ATLANTIC OCEAN

Red River

Mississippi River

AL

Savannah River

GA

ATLANTIC COASTAL PLAIN

Brazos River

MS

Alabama River

Chattahoochee River

TX

Colorado River

LA

30°N

EDWARDS PLATEAU

GULF COASTAL PLAIN

Mobile Bay

FL

Galveston Bay

Mississippi River Delta

Lake Okeechobee

Gulf of Mexico

BAHAMAS

Florida Keys

Straits of Florida

N
W E
S

CUBA

20°N

100°W

90°W

80°W

GH13

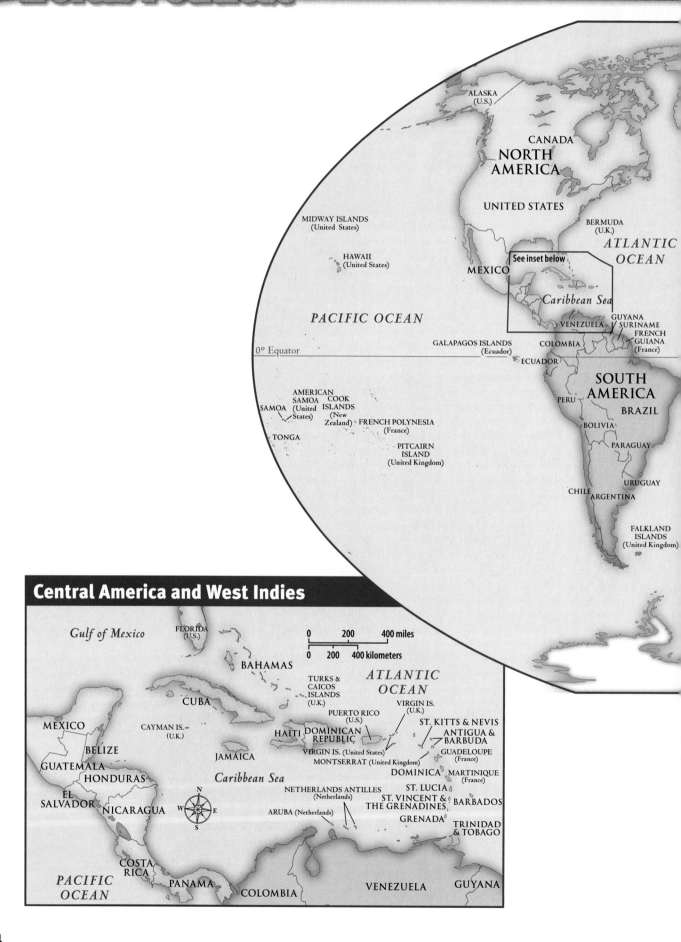

ALASKA
(U.S.)

CANADA

NORTH
AMERICA

UNITED STATES

MIDWAY ISLANDS
(United States)

BERMUDA
(U.K.)

ATLANTIC
OCEAN

See inset below

HAWAII
(United States)

MEXICO

Caribbean Sea

PACIFIC OCEAN

GUYANA
VENEZUELA SURINAME
FRENCH
GUIANA
(France)

GALAPAGOS ISLANDS
(Ecuador)

COLOMBIA

ECUADOR

0° Equator

AMERICAN
SAMOA   COOK
SAMOA (United ISLANDS
(United States) (New
States) Zealand) FRENCH POLYNESIA
(France)

TONGA

PITCAIRN
ISLAND
(United Kingdom)

SOUTH
AMERICA

PERU

BRAZIL

BOLIVIA

PARAGUAY

URUGUAY

CHILE
ARGENTINA

FALKLAND
ISLANDS
(United Kingdom)

Central America and West Indies

Gulf of Mexico

FLORIDA
(U.S.)

0   200   400 miles

0   200   400 kilometers

BAHAMAS

TURKS &
CAICOS
ISLANDS
(U.K.)

ATLANTIC
OCEAN

CUBA

VIRGIN IS.
(U.K.)

PUERTO RICO
(U.S.)

ST. KITTS & NEVIS

MEXICO

CAYMAN IS.
(U.K.)

HAITI DOMINICAN
REPUBLIC

ANTIGUA &
BARBUDA

BELIZE

JAMAICA

VIRGIN IS. (United States)
MONTSERRAT (United Kingdom)

GUADELOUPE
(France)

GUATEMALA

HONDURAS

Caribbean Sea

DOMINICA MARTINIQUE
(France)

EL
SALVADOR

N

NETHERLANDS ANTILLES
(Netherlands)

ST. LUCIA

ST. VINCENT &
THE GRENADINES

BARBADOS

NICARAGUA

W   E

ARUBA (Netherlands)

GRENADA

TRINIDAD
& TOBAGO

S

COSTA
RICA

PACIFIC
OCEAN

PANAMA

COLOMBIA

VENEZUELA

GUYANA

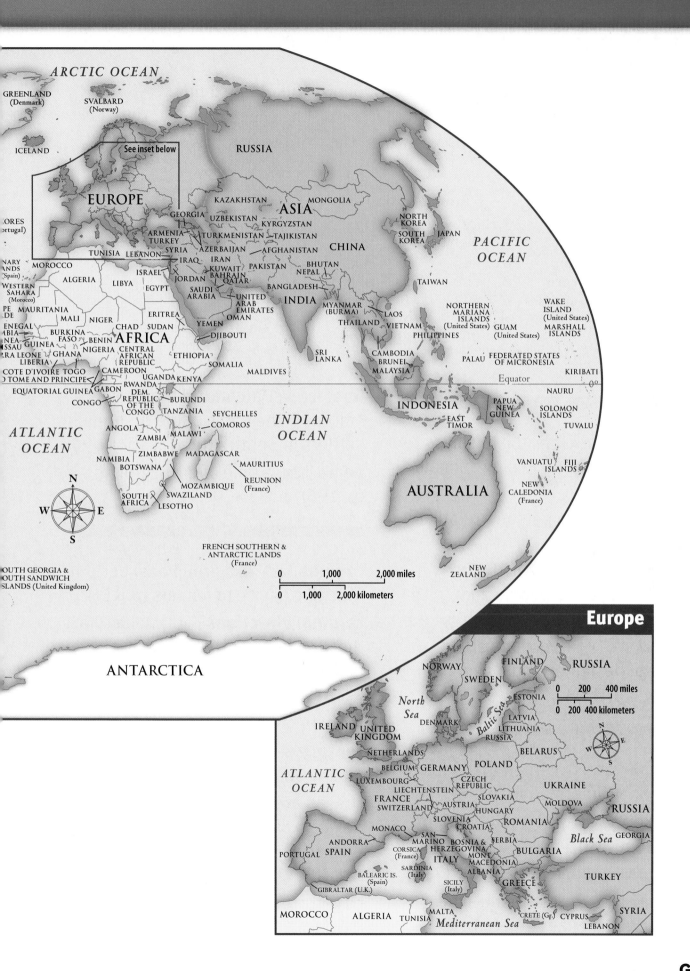

ARCTIC OCEAN

GREENLAND
(Denmark)

SVALBARD
(Norway)

ICELAND

RUSSIA

See inset below

EUROPE

ORES
ortugal)

GEORGIA

KAZAKHSTAN

ASIA

MONGOLIA

UZBEKISTAN

KYRGYZSTAN

NORTH
KOREA

ARMENIA
TURKEY

TURKMENISTAN

TAJIKISTAN

SOUTH
KOREA

JAPAN

PACIFIC
OCEAN

NARY
NDS
Spain)

MOROCCO

TUNISIA

AZERBAIJAN

LEBANON

SYRIA

IRAQ

IRAN

AFGHANISTAN

CHINA

ISRAEL

JORDAN

KUWAIT

BAHRAIN

PAKISTAN

BHUTAN
NEPAL

TAIWAN

WESTERN
SAHARA
(Morocco)

ALGERIA

LIBYA

EGYPT

QATAR

SAUDI
ARABIA

BANGLADESH

UNITED
ARAB
EMIRATES

INDIA

DE
PE
MAURITANIA

MALI

NIGER

CHAD

ERITREA

SUDAN

YEMEN

OMAN

MYANMAR
(BURMA)

LAOS

NORTHERN
MARIANA
ISLANDS
(United States)

WAKE
ISLAND
(United States)

ENEGAL
ABIA
NEA-
SSAU

GUINEA

BURKINA
FASO

BENIN

AFRICA

NIGERIA

DJIBOUTI

THAILAND

VIETNAM

GUAM
(United States)

MARSHALL
ISLANDS

RA LEONE

GHANA

CENTRAL
AFRICAN
REPUBLIC

ETHIOPIA

SRI
LANKA

CAMBODIA

PHILIPPINES

LIBERIA

COTE D'IVOIRE TOGO

CAMEROON

SOMALIA

MALDIVES

BRUNEI

PALAU

FEDERATED STATES
OF MICRONESIA

TOME AND PRINCIPE

UGANDA

KENYA

MALAYSIA

KIRIBATI

EQUATORIAL GUINEA

GABON

RWANDA

DEM.
REPUBLIC
OF THE
CONGO

Equator

0°

CONGO

BURUNDI

TANZANIA

INDIAN

INDONESIA

PAPUA
NEW
GUINEA

NAURU

ATLANTIC
OCEAN

ANGOLA

ZAMBIA

SEYCHELLES

COMOROS

OCEAN

EAST
TIMOR

SOLOMON
ISLANDS

TUVALU

MALAWI

NAMIBIA

ZIMBABWE

MADAGASCAR

MAURITIUS

VANUATU

FIJI
ISLANDS

BOTSWANA

N

W   E

S

SOUTH
AFRICA

MOZAMBIQUE

SWAZILAND

LESOTHO

REUNION
(France)

AUSTRALIA

NEW
CALEDONIA
(France)

OUTH GEORGIA &
OUTH SANDWICH
SLANDS (United Kingdom)

FRENCH SOUTHERN &
ANTARCTIC LANDS
(France)

0   1,000   2,000 miles

0   1,000   2,000 kilometers

NEW
ZEALAND

ANTARCTICA

NORWAY

FINLAND

RUSSIA

SWEDEN

ESTONIA

0   200   400 miles

North
Sea

Baltic Sea

0   200   400 kilometers

IRELAND

UNITED
KINGDOM

DENMARK

LATVIA

LITHUANIA

RUSSIA

N

NETHERLANDS

BELARUS

W   E

S

ATLANTIC
OCEAN

BELGIUM

GERMANY

POLAND

LUXEMBOURG

CZECH
REPUBLIC

UKRAINE

LIECHTENSTEIN

FRANCE

SWITZERLAND

AUSTRIA

SLOVAKIA

HUNGARY

MOLDOVA

RUSSIA

SLOVENIA

ROMANIA

MONACO

CROATIA

ANDORRA

SAN
MARINO

BOSNIA &
HERZEGOVINA

SERBIA

Black Sea

GEORGIA

PORTUGAL

SPAIN

CORSICA
(France)

ITALY

MONT.

BULGARIA

MACEDONIA

SARDINIA
(Italy)

ALBANIA

TURKEY

BALEARIC IS.
(Spain)

SICILY
(Italy)

GREECE

GIBRALTAR (U.K.)

MOROCCO

ALGERIA

TUNISIA

MALTA

CRETE (Gr.)

Mediterranean Sea

CYPRUS

SYRIA

LEBANON

GH15

Glossary

This Glossary will help you to pronounce and understand the meanings of the vocabulary in this book. The page number at the end of the definition tells you where the word first appears.

Pronunciation Key							
a	at	ī	ice	u	up	th	thin
ā	ape	î	pierce	ū	use	th	this
ä	far	o	hot	ü	rule	zh	measure
âr	care	ō	old	ů	pull	ə	about· taken·
e	end	ô	fork	ûr	turn		pencil· lemon·
ē	me	oi	oil	hw	white		circus
i	it	ou	out	ng	song		

A

agriculture (ag′ri kul′chər) the business of growing crops and raising animals (p. 115)

ancestor (an′ses tər) a person's relative from long ago (p. 82)

apartheid (ə pär′tād) South African policy forcing black people and white people to live apart (p. 105)

architecture (är′ki tek′chər) the art or science of designing and making buildings (p. 200)

B

bar graph (bär graf) a graph that uses bars to show information (p. 78)

barter (bär′ tər) to trade goods without using money (p. 64)

basin (bā′sin) a round lowland (p. 178)

bilingual (bī ling′gwəl) someone who speaks two languages (p. 82)

Boer (bôr) a Dutch word that means "farmer;" the name of the first Dutch settlers in South Africa (p. 104)

boom (büm) a time of quick growth (p. 196)

C

cabinet (kab′ə nit) a group of experts that give advice to leaders (p. 151)

cardinal directions (kär′də nal di rek′shəns) the directions north, south, east, and west (p. 100)

cash crops (kash krop) crops that farmers raise for money (p. 115)

century (sen′chə rē) a period of time lasting one hundred years (p. 28)

checks and balances (cheks and bal′ən sez) a system of government in which each branch of government can check, or stop, the work of the other (p. 111)

city-state (sit′ē stāt) a city that governs itself (p. 146)

civilization (siv′ə lə zā shən) a developed community (p. 23)

coastline (kōst′līn) land along an ocean or sea (p. 53)

communism (kom′yə niz′əm) a system in which property and goods are owned by the government and are to be shared equally by everyone (p. 189)

compass (kum′pəs) an instrument for showing directions (p. 184)

confederation (kən fed′ə rā′shən) a group of provinces or territories joined together (p. 66)

constitution (kän′stə tü′shən) a written plan of government (p. 31)

cooperate (kō op′ə rā′shən) to help each other (p. 203)

council (koun′səl) leaders of Italian regions who make laws (p. 149)

courtyard (kôrt′yärd) an open area surrounded by buildings (p. 202)

culture (kul′ chər) a way of life shared by a group of people (p. 44)

D

dam (dam) a wall or structure built across a river to hold back and control the water (p. 196)

deforestation (dē fôr′ist ā′shən) the destruction of forests (p. 196)

degree (di grē′) a unit of measuring distance on Earth's surface (p. 60)

democracy (di mok′rə sə) a country that has a government run by its people (p. 31)

designer (di zī′nər) a person who makes a plan for creating something (p. 155)

dynasty (dī′nə stē) ruling family in China (p. 183)

E

economy (i kon′ə mē) the way a country produces and uses its goods, natural resources, and services (p. 39)

empire (em′pīr) a group of lands that is led by an emperor or king (p. 143)

environment (en vī′rən mənt) the air, water, land, and other things that surround animals, people, and plants (p. 109)

equator (i kwā′tər) an imaginary line around the Earth halfway between the North Pole and the South Pole (p. 20)

executive branch (eg zek′ū tiv branch) the part of government that carries out laws (p. 32)

explorer (ek splôr′ ər) a person who goes to a place to find out about it (p. 24)

export (ek spôrt′) to send goods out of a country to be sold (p. 38)

extinct (ek stingkt′) no longer active or existing (p. 163)

F

factory (fak′tə rē) a place where a product is made (p. 38)

federal (fed′ər əl) a government where power is shared between the national and local levels (p. 70)

fiesta (fē es′tə) Spanish word for "party" (p. 45)

flow chart (flō chärt) a chart that shows the steps necessary to complete an activity (p. 158)

G

game reserve (gām ri zûrv′) land set aside for animals (p. 96)

geography (jē og′rə fē) the study of land and water and the way plants, people, and animals live on them (p. 14)

gorge (gôrj) a narrow valley between steep walls (p. 174)

graph (graf) a special kind of picture that shows information in a way that is easy to understand (p. 78)

grid (grid) lines that cross each other on a map (p. 60)

H

hacienda (hä′sē en′dē) large estates (p. 25)

hemisphere (hem′ is fîr) one half of Earth or another sphere (p. 20)

homeland (hōm′land′) the poorest parts of South Africa where blacks were forced to live during apartheid (p. 105)

##

immigrant (im′i grənt) a person who comes from one country to live in another (p. 41)

imperial (im pîr′ē əl) the system of emperor rule in China (p. 186)

import (im pôrt′) to bring in goods from another country to be sold (p. 38)

industry (in′də strē) a business that makes one kind of product (p. 73)

intermediate direction (in tər mēd′dē it di rek′shən) a direction halfway between two cardinal directions (p. 100)

international (in tər nash′ə nəl) involving different countries (p. 125)

international trade (in tər nash′ə nəl ′trād) trade between countries (p. 76)

J

judicial branch (jü dish′ əl branch) the part of government that decides if laws are fair and follow the constitution (p. 32)

L

latitude (lat′i tüd) a measure of distance north or south of the equator (p. 60)

legislative branch (lej′is lā tiv branch) the part of government that writes and passes new laws (p. 32)

land bridge (land brij) a strip of land connecting two larger pieces of land (p. 63)

land formation (land fôr mā′shən) the shapes of Earth's surface (p. 14)

line graph (līn graf) a graph that shows dots connected by lines to show change over time (p. 118)

livestock (līv′stok) animals raised on farms and ranches (p. 115)

longitude (lon´ ji tüd) a measure of distance east or west of the prime meridian (p. 60)

lowland (lō´lənd) an area that is lower than the land around it (p. 54)

M

manufacturing (man´yə fak´chər ing) making goods using machines (p. 73)

map scale (map skāl) the measurement a map uses to show the real distance between places on Earth (p. 180)

marionette (mar´ē ə net´) a puppet on strings (p. 165)

mineral (min´ər əl) a natural resource that is not a plant or animal (p. 36)

mountain pass (moun´tən pas) a steep road over a mountain (p. 140)

mountainous (moun´tə nəs) land that is steep and rocky (p. 134)

N

natural resource (nach´ər əl rē´sôrs) a material found in nature that people use (p. 36)

O

opera (op´ər ə) a musical play where all of the players sing their lines (p. 164)

P

pagoda (pə gō´də) old, wooden temples with graceful roofs that curve upwards (p. 200)

parliament (pär´ lə mənt) the legislative branch of Canada's government (p. 70)

patron (pā´trən) a person who supports art (p. 146)

peninsula (pə nin´sə lə) a long stretch of land with water all around it (p. 133)

plain (plān) an area of flat land (p. 14)

plateau (pla tō´) an area of flat land that is higher than the land around it (p. 14)

plaza (plä´zə) an open public square in a town or city (p. 43)

political party (pə lit´i kəl pär´tē) a group that directs government (p. 189)

pollution (pə lü´shən) when the environment is made dirty from harmful materials (p. 41)

porcelain (pôr´sə lin) fine, thin pottery (p. 184)

port (pôrt) a place where boats can bring their goods to land (p. 137)

prairie (prâr´ē) a flat or rolling land covered with grass (p. 58)

prehistoric (prē´his tōr´ik) a time before people wrote down history (p. 23)

prime meridian (prīm mə rid´ē ən) an imaginary line that runs from the North Pole to the South Pole through Greenwich, England (p. 20)

prime minister (prīm min´ə stər) the leader of the executive branch of Canada's government (p. 70)

product (prod´ukt) anything that is made or created (p. 73)

province (prov′ins) one of the political areas that make up a country (p. 66)

R

rain forest (rān fôr′ist) thick forests that receive a large amount of rain (p. 15)

rebel (re bəl′) to fight back (p. 186)

region (rē jen) an area with common features (p. 54)

renaissance (ren′ə säns) Italian word for "rebirth;" describes the rebirth or Italian culture in the 1300s and 1400s (p. 147)

republic (ri pub′lik) a nation without a king or queen (p. 26)

resort (ri zôrt′) a special hotel for tourists (p. 157)

revolution (rev ə lü′shən) the overthrowing of a government (p. 27)

road map (rōd map) a map that shows the roads of a given area (p. 140)

ruins (rü′inz) an old building that has fallen apart over time (p. 133)

S

safari (sə fär′ē) a trip to an African game reserve (p. 96)

sphere (sfîr) an object that is round, like a ball (p. 20)

steppe (step) dry, windy lands (p. 177)

T

technology (tek nol′ə jē) the knowledge and skills to make new things (p. 193)

territory (ter′i tôr′ē) one of the political areas that make up a country over which the national government has more control (p. 66)

time line (tīm līn) a list that tells the order of important events (p. 28)

tourist (tür′ist) a person who travels to different places for enjoyment (p. 84)

tournament (tür′nə mənt) a series of games (p. 124)

translate (trans lāt′) to rewrite in another language (p. 165)

tundra (tun′drə) a flat area of frozen land without trees (p. 56)

tunnel (tun′əl) a wide road for cars and trucks (p. 140)

V

veld (velt) wide, flat areas usually covered in grass and low bushes (p. 93)

village (vil′ij) a small community where people live (p. 138)

volcano (vol kā′nō) an opening in the Earth's surface through which hot rocks and ash are forced out (p. 14)

Index

This index lists many topics that appear in the book, along with the pages on which they are found. Page numbers after an *m* refer you to a map.

A

Adobe homes, 18
Africa, m6, m21. *See also* South Africa
African Bush Elephants, 97
Agriculture and farming
 in ancient Rome, 145
 in Canada, 54–55, 75, 76
 in China, 174, 177, 178, 195
 defined, 115
 in Italy, 134, 135, 136, 152, 153
 in Mexico, 18, 23, 35, 36
 in South Africa, 94, 105, 115
Alamo, battle of, 27
Alberta, Canada, m66
Alligators, 17
Alps mountain range, 134, 135
Ancestors, 82
Animals
 of Canada, 55, 57, 59
 of China, 176, 177, 178, 194
 of Italy, 134, 153
 of Mexico, 13, 16, 17, 25, 35
 of South Africa, 96, 103, 115
Anise, 193
Anne of Green Gables (Montgomery), 51, 82
Antarctica, *m21*
Apartheid, 105, 114, 123
Apartheid Museum, 121
Apennines mountain range, 134, 135
Apulia, Italy, 149
Arabia, *m193*

Architecture and buildings, 144, 147, 200
Arctic, 56, 57
Arno River, Florence, 136
Arts and artists
 in China, 200, 201
 in Italy, 146, 156, 164
 in Mexico, 44
Asia, m21, 41, m193
Atlantic Ocean, m21
Augustus, 144
Aztec Indians
 Calendar Stone, 4, 23
 and Cortés, 24, 28
 Floating Gardens, 42
 Templo Mayor pyramid, 43

B

Bald eagles, 57
Ballet Folklórico de Mexico, 44
Bamboo, 178, 185
Banff, Canada, 81
Baobab trees, 96, 97
Bar graphs, 78–79
Barnard, Christiaan, 90, 122
Bartering, 64
Basins, 178
Baths of Rome, 144
Bats, 17
Battle of the Alamo, 27
Beans, 35, 36
Bears, 16
Beavers, 58, 64
Beijing, China
 archaeology near, 183
 as capital city, 174
 and Khanbaliq, 170
 living in, 204–5
 maps, m173, m181
Belize, 13, m15

Bellas Artes Palace, 44
Bilingualism, 82
Bill of Rights in South Africa, 109
Birds, 16, 17
Bloemfontein, South Africa, *m93, m95, m101,* 111
Bobcats, 16
Boers, 104
Bo-Kaap neighborhood of Cape Town, South Africa, 124
Booms, 196, 197
Botswana, *m93, m101*
Brazil, 175
British Columbia, Canada, m66
Brunelleschi, 147
Buildings and architecture, 144, 147, 200
Butterflies, 13

C

Cabinets, 151
Cabot, John, 63
Cacao, 36
Cactus plants, 16
Caesar, Julius, 130, 143
Calendar stone of the Aztecs, 23
Calgary, Canada, 83, 84, 85
Calgary Stampede, 84
California, 27
Calligraphy, 201
Campbell, Kim, 70
Camps Bay, Cape Town, South Africa, 117
Canada
 capital, 54, *m75*
 constitution, 69, 71
 culture, 84

economy, 72–77
geography, 52–59
government, 68–71
history, 62–67
living in, 80–85
maps, *m5, m54, m56, m64, m65, m66, m74–75*
national symbols, 55, 58, 69, 71
natural resources, *m74–75, 74–75*
population, 78–79, 83, 175
tourism in, 84
Canada Olympic Park, 85
Canadian-Pacific Railway, 67, 70, 77
Canadian Shield, 56–57, 63
Cape Peninsula, South Africa, 125
Cape Town, South Africa
 about, 122–23
 Camps Bay, 117
 coastline, 94
 founder, 104
 heart transplant in, 90
 as legislative capital, 108, 111
 maps, *m95*
Cape Town International Jazz Festival, 125
Capitals
 of Canada, 54, *m75*
 of China, 174, 204
 of Italy, 150
 of Mexico, 41 (*see also* Mexico City)
 of South Africa, 111
Cardinal directions, 100–101
Cars, 114

Cartier, Jacques, 64, 82
Cash crops, 115. *See also* Agriculture and farming
Castle of Good Hope (building), 122
Cedar trees, 74
Celebrations, 45
Central Plains, 58
Centuries, 28
Chamber of Deputies, 150
Champlain, Samuel de, 50, 64
Chapultepec Park, Mexico City, 42
Chart and graph skills
  bar graphs, 78–79
  flow charts, 158–59
  line graphs, 118–19
  time lines, 28–29
Checks and balances, 111
Cheese, 153, 158
Cheetahs, 97
Chickens, 35
Children's rights in Mexico, 33
China
  calligraphy, 201
  capital, 174, 204
  culture, 190, 198–205
  economy, 38, 192–97
  geography, 172–79
  government, 188–91
  Great Wall, *m184*, 184–85
  history, 182–87
  living in, 198–205
  maps, *m8, m173, m181, m184, m193*
  population, 175, 197
  tourism in, 156, 196
China (porcelain), 184, 193, 200
Chinese New Year, 199
Christian religion, 25
Citizenship, 196
City-States, 146
Civilization, 23
Cixi, Empress dowager of China, 171

Climates
  in Canada, 56
  in China, 173, 178
  in Mexico, 18
Clothing, 154, 194–95
Coal, 194
Coastlines
  of Canada, 53
  of China, 174, 195
  of Italy, 136, 137
Coffee, 35, *m37*
Colonies, 64, 66
Colosseum, 142, 143
Columbus, Christopher, 137
Communism, 187, 189, 190
Company Gardens, 122
Compasses, 184
Compass rose, 100–101
Concrete, 145
Confederations, 66
Confucious, 190, 201
Constitution Plaza of Mexico City, 43
Constitutions
  of Canada, 69, 71
  of Mexico, 27, 29, 31, 32, 35
  of South Africa, 109
Cooperation, 203
Copper, 75, 113
Corn, 35, 36
Cortés, Hernán, 24, 28
Cotton, 35, 36
Council of Ministers, 151
Councils, 149
Courtyards, 202
Cows, 35
Crafts
  of China, 200
  of Italy, 154, 155
  of Mexico, 39
Cricket, 124
Culture
  of Canada, 84
  of China, 190, 198–205
  defined, 44
  of Italy, 164
  of Mexico City, 44–45

Cypress trees, 134

Dams, 196, 197
Dancing, 44
Deer, 57
Deforestation, 196
De Klerk, F. W., 105
Democracy, 31, 189
Deserts
  of China, 177
  of Mexico, 14, 16, 18
  of South Africa, 94
Designers, 155
Diamonds, 98, 113
Dolomites mountain range, 134
Dolores, Mexico, 10
Donkeys, 25
Drakensberg Mountains, South Africa, 95
Ducal Palace, Mantua, 131
Dumplings, 199
Durban, South Africa, 112, 121
Dynasties, 183, 187

Eagles, 57
Earthquakes, 43
Eastern Cape, South Africa, *m95*
Economy
  of Canada, 72–77
  of China, 192–97
  defined, 39
  of Italy, 152–57
  of Mexico, 34–39
  of South Africa, 112–17
Edmonton, Canada, 83
Education, 70, 82, 190–91
Ejidos, 35
Elections, 91, 106–7, 189
Elephants, 6, 97
Elizabeth II, 71
El Salvador, *m15*
Emperors, 170, 182, 183, 205

Empires, 143, 183, 186
England
  See also Great Britain
  and Canada, 64, 65
  explorers from, 63, 64
  Queen of England, 69, 71
Environment, 109, 196, 197
Equator, 20
Europe, *m7, m21*, 41, 133
Executive branches
  in Mexican government, 32
  in South African government, 110, 111
Explorers
  in Canada, 63, 64–65
  in Mexico, 24
Exports
  of Canada, 76
  of Mexico, 38
  of South Africa, 113
Extinction, 163

Factories
  in China, 192, 196
  in Mexico, 38
  in South Africa, 114
Families, 161, 202, 203
Farming. *See* Agriculture and farming
Federal government, 70
Festivals, 199
Fiestas, 45
Fir trees, 59
Fishing
  in Canada, 75
  in China, 174, 195
  in Italy, 137
Floating Gardens, 42
Floodplains, 174
Florence, Italy, 136, 146, 147, 156
Flow charts, 158–59
Food
  See also Agriculture and farming

in China, 178, 195, 199, 203, 204
in Italy, 139, 153, 154, 155, 161
Forbidden City, 205
Forests
in Canada, 56, 57, 59, 73, 74
in China, 194, 196
and deforestation, 196
Forum of Rome, 130
Foxes, 55
France
and Canada, 64, 82
explorers from, 50, 64
and South Africa, 104
tourism in, 156
Freedom Day in South Africa, 107
French and Indian War, 65
French language, 82
Frida Kahlo Museum, 11
Frogs, 17
Fur trade, 64

Galleria Vittorio Emanuele II, 138
Game reserves, 96
Geese, 57
Genoa, Italy, 137
Geography
about, 14
of Canada, 52–59
of China, 172–79
of Italy, 132–39
of Mexico, 12–19
of South Africa, 93–99
Germany, 104
Ginger, 193
Giraffes, 97
Gobi Desert, 177
Gold
in Canada, 70, 75
in Mexico, 25, 36
in South Africa, 99, 113
Golden monkeys, 178
Golden Rule, 201
Goods, 195

Gorges, 174
Government
of Canada, 68–71
of China, 188–91
of Italy, 147, 148–51
of Mexico, 30–33
of South Africa, 105, 108–11
Governors, 32
Grapes, 153
Graphs, 78–79
Gray wolves, 57
Great Britain, 65, 104, 186
Greater St. Lucia Wetlands Park, 116
Great Hall of the People in Beijing, 188
Great Lakes, 53, 54
Great Plains, 58
Great Wall of China, m184, 184–85
Greece, ancient, 133, 135, 143, 147, 162
Greenland, m66
Groote Schuur Hospital, Cape Town, 90
Guadalajara, Mexico, 41
Guatemala, 13, m15
Gulf of Mexico, m15, m37

Haciendas, 25, 35
Hainan, China, 174
Harbors, 112, 137
Heart transplants, 90, 122
Hemispheres, 20–21, m21
Hickory trees, 55
Hidalgo, Miguel, 10, 26, 28
Hiking, 124
Hills, 134
Himalayan Mountains, 176
Hockey Hall of Fame, 81
Holland, 104, 122
Homelands, 105
Hong Kong, China, m173, 174, m181, 186
Horses, 25
Horseshoe Falls, 54
Huangguoshu waterfall, 172

Huang He river, 174
Hudson, Henry, 65
Hudson Bay, 65, m66
Hydropower, 196, 197

Ice carvings, 84
Immigrants, 41
Imperial City, 205
Imperialism, 186
Imperial Palace, 171, 205
Imports, 38, 76
Independence Day (Mexico), 10
India, 104, m173, m181, m193
Indian Ocean, m93
Indian ruins, 39
Industry, 73, 197
The Innocents Abroad (Twain), 163
Insects, 13, 16, 17
Intermediate directions, 100–101
International (defined), 125
International trade, 76–77
Inuit, 57, 84
Iron, 75
Isabella d'Este, 131
Italy
capital, 150
culture, 164
economy, 152–57
geography, 132–39
government, 147, 148–51
history, 142–47
living in, 160–65
maps, m7, m133, m141
population, 138
tourism in, 156, 157, 163

Jacob, Erasmus, 98
Jaguars, 17
Japan, 38

Johannesburg, South Africa, m93, m95, m101, 121
Juárez, Benito, 29
Judicial branches
in Mexican government, 32
in South African government, 110, 111

Kahlo, Frida, 11, 44
Kalahari Desert, South Africa, 94, m95
Karst landscapes, 179
Khanbaliq, 170
Khoikhoi, 103, 122
Kimberley, South Africa, m93, m101
King, Martin Luther, 106
King Protea flowers, 96, 97
Kites, 185
Kruger National Park, 96, 97
Kublai Khan, 170, 183
Kung fu, 198
Kunlun mountains, m173

Land bridge, 63
Land formations, 14, m15, 53
Leatherback turtles, 97
Legionnaires, 143
Legislative branches
in Mexican government, 32
in South African government, 110, 111, 123
Leonardo Da Vinci, 146
Lesotho, m93, m101
Line graphs, 118–19
Little Red Book, 190
Livestock, 115, 153
Lizards, 16
Logging, 73, 74
Lowlands, 54–55

Index

Macau, China, m173, 174
Main Temple in Mexico City, 43
Mandela, Nelson
    and apartheid, 105
    in Cape Town, 122
    and constitution, 109
    as president, 91, 106, 107
Manitoba, Canada, m66
Mantua city-state, 131
Manufacturing, 73
Mao Zedong, 190
Maple trees, 55
Map skills
    hemispheres, 20–21
    intermediate directions, 100–101
    map scale, 180–81
    road maps, 140–41
Mariachis, 45
Marionettes, 165
Maya Indians, 23, 35
Medici family, 146
Mediterranean Sea, 133, 143, 153
Metropolitan Cathedral (Mexico City), 43
Mexican American War, 27, 28
Mexican Indians, 35
Mexican Revolution of 1910, 27, 29
Mexican War of Independence, 26, 28, 31
Mexico
    capital, 41 (see also Mexico City)
    constitution, 27, 29, 32, 35
    economy, 34–39
    flag, 31
    geography, m4, 12–19
    government, 30–33
    history, 22–27, 28–29
    living in, 40–45

maps, m4, m13, m15, m21
    tourism in, 39, 42
Mexico City
    as capital, 41
    culture, 44–45
    downtown, 43
    factories, 38
    living in, 40–45
    maps, m4, m15
    National Palace, 30, 43
    and New Spain, 24
    in Plateau of Mexico, 14
    and tourism, 39
Middle Ages, 146
Middle East, 41
Minerals
    about, 98
    in Canada, 75
    in China, 194
    in Mexico, 25, 36
    in South Africa, 98, 113, 118–19
Ming Dynasty, 184, 185
Ming Tombs, 205
Mining
    See also Minerals
    in Canada, 75
    in South Africa, 98–99, 113, 122
Moctezuma, 24
Monarch butterflies, 13
Monarch Butterfly Biosphere Reserve, 13
Mongolia, 170, m173, 177, m181, m193, 202
Monkeys, 17
Montgomery, Lucy Maud, 51, 82
Montreal, Canada, 55, 64, 81, 82, 83
Mooncakes, 199
Moose, 57
Mountain lions, 16
Mountains
    of Canada, 58
    of China, 176
    of Italy, 134, 135, 162, 163

of Mexico, 14
    mountainous (defined), 134
    mountain passes, 140
    of South Africa, 93, 99
Mount Vesuvius, 162, 163
Mozambique, m93, m101
Mozzarella cheese, 153
Mt. Etna, 135
Mt. Everest, m173, 176
Mulberry trees, 174, 194
MuseuMAfricA, 121
Museum of Fine Arts in Montreal, 84
Music
    in China, 200
    in Italy, 164
    in Mexico, 45
    in South Africa, 125

Namibia, m93, m101
Naples, Italy, 162–63
Napolitano, Giorgio, 151
Narwhales, 57
National government of Mexico, 32
Nationalists of China, 187
National Museum of Anthropology in Mexico City, 42
National Palace of Mexico City, 30, 43
Native Americans, 57
Natural resources
    of Canada, m74–75, 74–75
    of China, 194
    of Mexico, 36, m37
    of South Africa, 98–99, 115, 118–19
Nature, 201
Nevada, 27
New Brunswick, Canada, 66, m66
Newfoundland, Canada, 63, 71, 75
New Spain, 24
Niagara River, 54

Noordhoek, South Africa, 94
North America, m4, m5, 13, m21
Northern Cape of South Africa, m95
North Korea, m173, m181
Nova Scotia, Canada, 66, m66
Nunavut, Canada, m66, 67, 71

Oak trees, 55
Oaxaca, Mexico, 39
Oil, 36, m37
Olives, 153
Olympics, 85, 204
Ontario, Canada, 66, m66
Opera, 164
Orange River, South Africa, 95, m95, 98
O. R. Tambo International Airport, 117
Ostriches, 97, 115
Ottawa, Canada, 54, m66, 83
Oxen, 25

Pacific Ocean, m21
Pagodas, 200
Pakistan, m173, m181
Palio Festival, 157
Pandas, 178
Parliament
    about, 70
    in Canada, 70
    in Italy, 150, 151
    in South Africa, 110, 111, 123
Parmesan cheese, 158
Parroquia de Nuestra Senora de Dolore, 10
Parties, 189
Passeggiata, 161
Patrons, 146
Peking Roast Duck, 204

Penguins, 97, 125
Peninsulas, 133
Piazzas, 139, 162
Pincushion flowers, 97
Pine trees, 59, 74
Pinocchio, 165
Pizza Margherita, 162
Place des Arts, 82
Plains
    of China, 177
    of Italy, 134
    of Mexico, 14
    of South Africa, 93
Plants
    See also Agriculture and
    farming
    of Canada, 55, 57, 59, 74
    of China, 178, 179, 194
    of Mexico, 16, 17, 18, 19
    of South Africa, 94, 96,
    97
Plateaus
    of China, 176
    of Mexico, 14, *m15,* 18,
    36, 41
    of South Africa, 93
Platinum, 113
Plazas, 43
Polar bears, 57
Political parties, 189
Pollution, 41, 197
Polo, Marco, 170, 204
Pompeii, 162
Ponte Vecchio, 136
Population
    of Brazil, 175
    of Canada, 78–79, 83,
    175
    of China, 175, 197
    of Italy, 138
    of Russia, 175
    of United States, 175
Porcelain, 184, 193, 200
Po River Valley, 135, 153
Port Elizabeth, South
    Africa, *m95*
Ports, 137, 163
Pottery, *m37,* 154, 184,
    193

Poverty, 189
Prairie dogs, 16
Prairies, 58, 75
Prehistoric groups, 23
Presidents, 149, 150, 151
Pretoria, South Africa,
    m93, 100–101, *m101,*
    111
Prime meridian, 20
Prime Minister, 70, 151
Prince Edward Island, 51,
    m66
Prodi, Romano, 151
Products, 73
Provinces, 66, 70
Puebla, Mexico, 41
Pyramids, 23, 43

Q

Qin Dynasty, 183
Qing Dynasty, 186
Quebec, Canada
    map, 66, *m66*
    population, 55, 79
    settlers, 50, 64
Queen of England, 69, 71
Quetzals, 17

R

Railroads
    in Canada, 67, 70, 77
    in China, 196
Rain forests, *m15,* 17, 19
Rain Queen, 103
Raphael, 146
Rebels, 186
Red Guard, 190
Re-education, 190
Regions, 54, 149
Religion, 25
Renaissance, 131, 147
Republics, 26
Reserves, 178
Resorts, 157
Revolutions, 27, 187
Rhodes, Cecil, 122
Rhodes scholarship, 122
Rice, 174, 178, 195

Riebeeck, Jan van, 104
Rights, 69
Rio Grande River, *m13*
Rivera, Diego, 11, 44
Rivers, 136, 174, 196, 197
Road maps, 140–41
Roadrunners, 16
Roads, 144, 145
Robben Island Prison,
    South Africa, 91
Rocky Mountains, 58
Rodeos, 84
Roman Empire
    Colosseum, 142
    end of, 146
    Forum, 130
    growth of, 143
    living in, 144–45
    and Pompeii, 162
    and Renaissance, 147
Rome, Italy, 134, 136, 150,
    156
Rosewood trees, 16
Rossini, Gioacchino, 164
Royal Winnipeg Ballet, 84
Rugby, 124
Ruins, 39, 133, 156, 162
Rural life, 202
Russia, 175

S

Safaris, 96, 116
Saguaro cactus, 16
San, 103, 122
San Marino, 135
Sardinia, Italy, 135, 157
Saskatchewan, Canada,
    m66
"The School of Athens"
    (Raphael), 146
Senate, 150
Service industry, 39, 73
Settlers, 25
Seven Years' War, 65
Shakaland, 116
Shanghai, China, *m173,*
    174, 180, *m181*
Sheep, 35
Shoes, 154, 155

Sichuan Basin, *m173,* 178
Sicily, Italy, 135, 157
Silk
    from China, 174, 193,
    194–95, 200
    from Italy, 154
    making silk clothing,
    194–95
Silk Road, 193, *m193*
Silver
    in Canada, 75
    in Mexico, 25, 36, *m37*
    in South Africa, 113
Snakes, 16, 17
Soccer, 124, 165
South Africa
    agriculture, 105, 115
    capital, 111
    cities, 121–23
    constitution, 109
    economy, 112–17
    elections, 91, 106–7
    geography, 93–99
    government, 105,
    108–11
    history, 102–7
    living in, 120–25
    maps, *m6, m93, m95,*
    m101, m115
    natural resources,
    98–99, *m115,* 118–19
    plants, 94, 96, 97
    tourism in, 116–17
    wildlife, 96, 97
South America, *m21*
Spain, 24–25, 28, 35, 156
Spheres, 20
Spider monkeys, 17
Sports
    in ancient Rome, 143
    in Canada, 85
    in Italy, 165
    in South Africa, 124
Spruce trees, 59
State government of
    Mexico, 32
Steppes, 177
St. Lawrence Lowlands,
    m54, 54–55

Index

St. Lawrence River, 50, 64
Stone Forest, 179
Sugarcane, 25
Summer Palace, 205
Swaziland, *m93*

Table Mountain, Cape
    Town, South Africa, 124
Taipei, Taiwan, m173, 174,
    m181
Taiping Rebellion, 186
Taiwan, *m173,* 174, *m181*
Taklimakan Desert, *m173*
Tarantulas, 16
Tea, 193, 194
Technology, 193, 208
Temples, 145, 205
Templo Mayor (Aztec
    pyramid), 43
Tenochtitlán, 24, 28
Terracotta soldiers, 182
Territories, 66
Texas, 27
Three Gorges Dam, 197
Tiananmen Square, 205
Tibet, m173, 176
Time lines, 28–29
Tools, 183
Toronto, Ontario, 55, *m66,*
    81, 83
Tourism
    in Canada, 84

in China, 156, 196
in Italy, 156, 157, 163
in Mexico, 39, 42
in South Africa, 116–17
Tournaments, 124
Towns, 138
Trade
    See also Economy
    of Canada, 64, 76–77
    of China, 186, 193, 196
Traditions, 199
Trans-Canada highway, 77
Translations, 165
Transplants, 90, 122
Transportation
    in Canada, 77
    in China, 196, 202, 203,
        204
    in South Africa, 114
Trees, 17, 19, 96
Trevi fountain, Rome, 164
Tundra, 56
Tunnels, 140–41, *m141*
Turtles, 97
Tuscany, Italy, 134, 154
Twain, Mark, 163

Umbria, Italy, 149
Underground Dragon, 204
United States
    and Canada, 76
    government, 151

and Mexico, 13, 27, 38
    population, 175
    tourism, 156
    trade, 38, 196
Utah, 27

Valley of Mexico, 23
Vancouver, Canada, 81
Vaporettos, 136
Velds, 93
Veneto, Italy, 149
Venice, Italy, 136, 146
Victoria and Alfred
    Waterfront in Cape
    Town, South Africa, 123
Vietnam, *m173, m181*
Vikings, 63
Villages, 138, 139, 174,
    202
Vinland, 63
Volcanos
    of Italy, 162, 163
    of Mexico, 14, 15

Walnut trees, 16, 55
War of Independence
    (Mexico), 26, 28, 31
Water systems, 144
Wealth, 189
Weather, 153
Western Cape, South

Africa, 94, *m95*
Whales, 57
Wheels, 25
Wildlife. See Animals
Wine, 154
Witwatersrand mountain
    range, 99
Wolong Panda Reserve,
    178
Wolves, 57
Women, 191
Wood products, 73
Woolen cloth, 159
World Cup soccer, 124, 165
World Trade Organization,
    196

Yaks, 176
Yangtze River, 174, 197
Yellow Crane Pagoda, 200
Yuan (money), 196
Yukon Territory, Canada,
    m66, 70
Yunnan province, 179
Yurts, 202, 203

Zacatecas, 36
Zimbabwe, *m93, m101*
Zocalo (Constitution
    Plaza), 43
Zulu, 104, 110, 116

Maps: XNR.

Illustrations: 17 John Megahan; 23 Nicole Tadgell; 24-25 Sonja Lamut; 51 Gary Overacre; 143 Angus McBride; 144-145 Ellen Beier; 158-159 Necdet Yilmaz

Photography Credits: All Photographs are by Macmillan/McGraw-hill (MMH) except as noted below.

Raymond Gehman/CORBIS; vi (bl)SuperStock, (br)David Sanger Photography/Alamy; viii Keren Su/CORBIS; ix Ian Dagnall/Alamy; 2 (cl)Ron Chapple/Getty Images, (b)Bill Bachmann/Alamy; 3 (tl)David Lyons/Alamy, (tr)Xinhua/Landov, (b)Michael Meyersfeld/Masterfile; 4 (bl)SCPhotos/Alamy, (tr)Danny Lehman/CORBIS; 5 (tr)Alaska Stock LLC/Alamy, (br)Images Etc Ltd/Alamy; 6 (tr)Nigel J. Dennis; Gallo Images/CORBIS, (bl)imagebroker/Alamy; 7 (tr)C Squared Studios/Getty Images, (bl)Art Kowalsky/Alamy; 8 (tr)KATHERINE FENG/GLOBIO/Minden Pictures, (b)Digital Vision/PunchStock; 9 Wolfgang Kaehler/Alamy; 10 (tl)The Granger Collection, New York, (tr)Danny Lehman/CORBIS, (b)Reuters/CORBIS; 11(tl)Bettmann/CORBIS, (tr)Lightworks Media/Alamy, (br)2007 Banco de México Diego Rivera & Frida Kahlo Museums Trust. Av. Cinco de Mayo No. 2, Col. Centro, Del. Cuauhtémoc 06059, México, D.F. and Art Resource, NY, (bl)2007 Banco de México Diego Rivera & Frida Kahlo Museums Trust. Av. Cinco de Mayo No. 2, Col. Centro, Del. Cuauhtémoc 06059, México, D.F. and THE BRIDGEMAN ART LIBRARY; 12-13 Danny Lehman/CORBIS; 12 (bcl)David Muench/CORBIS, (bcr)Papilio/Alamy, (br)Russell Gordon/DanitaDelimont.com.; 13 (t)Ingram Publishing/Alamy, (b)BRUCE COLEMAN INC./Alamy; 14-15 Sergio Dorantes/CORBIS; 14 David Muench/CORBIS; 15 (t)SAS/Alamy, (b)AA World Travel Library/Alamy; 16 (t)GERRY ELLIS/Minden Pictures, (c)Papilio/Alamy, (b)David A. Barnes/Alamy; 17 (t)MICHAEL & PATRICIA FOGDEN/Minden Pictures, (b)Garry DeLong/Alamy, (br)SCPhotos/Alamy; 18 (t)Peter Donaldson/Alamy, (b)Catherine Karnow/CORBIS; 19 (t)Russell Gordon/DanitaDelimont.com, (b)Danny Lehman/CORBIS; 22-23 Witold Skrypczak/LPI; 22 (bl)Danny Lehman/CORBIS, (bc)Richard T. Nowitz/CORBIS, (br)Wendy Connett/Alamy; 23 Danny Lehman/CORBIS; 24 The Art Archive/Palazzo Pitti Florence; 25 Richard T. Nowitz/CORBIS; 26 (t)Wendy Connett/Alamy, (b)Morton Beebe/CORBIS; 27(t)The Granger Collection, New York, (b)Witold Skrypczak/LPI; 28 (t) (br)The Granger Collection, New York, (bl)The Art Archive/Palazzo Pitti Florence/Dagli Orti (A); 29-30 JTB Photo Communications, Inc./Alamy; 29 (l)The Granger Collection, New York.; (r)Superstock; 30 (bl)SuperStock, (br)Keith Dannemiller/CORBIS; 31 SuperStock; 33 (t)Keith Dannemiller/CORBIS, (b)JTB Photo Communications, Inc./Alamy; 34-35 Bob Krist/CORBIS; 34 (bl)Jeff Greenberg/Photo Edit, Inc., (bc)Index Stock/Alamy, (br)Russell Gordon/ DanitaDelimont.com; 35 Jeff Greenberg/Photo Edit, Inc.; 36 (l)Jan Butchofsky-Houser/CORBIS, (b) ImageState/Alamy; 37 (tl)Phil Schermeister/CORBIS, (tr)Index Stock/Alamy, (bl)Douglas Peebles/CORBIS, (bc)Dave G. Houser/Corbis; 38-39 Ian Dagnall/Alamy; 39 (t) (cl)Russell Gordon/ DanitaDelimont.com, (cr)Bob Krist/CORBIS; 40 (bl)David Young Wolff/ Photo Edit, Inc., (bc)David R. Frazier Photolibrary, Inc./Alamy, (br)Bill Bachmann/ DantiaDelimont.com; 41 David Young Wolff/Photo Edit, Inc.; 42 (tl)David R. Frazier Photolibrary, Inc./Alamy, (b)World Pictures/Alamy, (tr)Peter Horree/Alamy; 43 (t)Jon Arnold Images/Alamy, (b)Nik Wheeler/CORBIS; 44 (t)Bettmann/CORBIS, (b)Robert Fried/Alamy; 45 (t)Bill Bachmann/ DantiaDelimont.com, (b)Jon Arnold Images/Alamy; 48 (t)Creatas/PictureQuest; 49 Yves Marcoux/First Light/Getty Images; 50 (tr)Bill Brooks/Alamy, (cl)North Wind Picture Archives/Alamy, (c)The Granger Collection, New York; 51 (tr)Grant Faint/The Image Bank/GettyImages, (c)Jan Butchofsky-Houser/CORBIS; 52-53 Bill Brooks/Alamy; 52 (bl)Bill Brooks/Alamy, (bcl)James Smedley/Getty Images/First Light, (bcr)Alaska Stock LLC/Alamy, (br)Bill Stormont/CORBIS; 53 (t)Stephen Saks Photography/Alamy, (b)Bill Brooks/Alamy; 54 Hisham Ibrahim/Photographer's Choice/Getty Images; 55 (t)Robert Harding Picture Library Ltd/Alamy, (cr)James Smedley/Getty Images/First Light, (br)Robert McGouey/Alamy; 56 (tl)Copyright PATRICIO ROBLES GIL/SIERRA MADRE/Minden Pictures, (b)YVA MOMATIUK/JOHN EASTCOTT/Minden Pictures, (cr)Nicholas Reuss/Lonely Planet Images ; 57 (tr)Hemis/Alamy, (cr)Wolfgang Kaehler/CORBIS, (b)Alaska Stock LLC/Alamy; 58 (cl)Dynamic Graphics Group/Creatas/Alamy, (b)Bill Stormont/CORBIS; 59 (t)Raymond Gehman/CORBIS, (cr)Bill Brooks/Alamy; 62-63 North Wind Picture Archives; 62 (t)tbkmedia.de/Alamy, (bc) (bl)The Granger Collection, New York; 63 (tr)The Granger Collection, New York, (br)The Bridgeman Art Library; 64 The Granger Collection, New York; 65 North Wind Picture Archives; 67 (t)tbkmedia.de/Alamy, (cr)North Wind Picture Archives, (b)Images Etc Ltd/Alamy, (bkgd)North Wind Picture Archives; 68-69 Fotostock Int./Superstock;

68 (bl)Digital Archive Japan/Alamy, (br)Michael Mahovlich/Masterfile; 69 Digital Archive Japan/Alamy; 70 (tl)Private Collection/Peter Newark American Pictures/The Bridgeman Art Library, (c)Hulton-Deutsch Collection/CORBIS, (bl)VANCOUVER SUN/CORBIS SYGMA; 71 (t)Digital Archive Japan/Alamy, (tr)Ron Poling, Canadian Press/AP Photo, (cr)Fotostock Int./Superstock, (bl)Michael Mahovlich/Masterfile; 72-73 Gunter Marx Photography/CORBIS; 72 (bl)AP Photo, (bc)Radius Images/Alamy, (br)Gunter Marx Photography/CORBIS; 73 (cr)AP Photo, (br)Arco Images/Alamy; 74 Christopher J. Morris/CORBIS; 75 (tl)Radius Images/Alamy, (tr)Lloyd Sutton/Masterfile, (br)Gunter Marx/Alamy; 76 Gunter Marx Photography/CORBIS; 77 (tl)Wolfgang Kaehler/CORBIS, (tr)Phil Degginger/Alamy, (cr)Gunter Marx Photography/CORBIS; 79 J. A. Kraulis/Masterfile; 80-81Michael Klinec/Alamy; 80 (bl)Rudy Sulgan/Corbis, (bc)Bob Krist/CORBIS, (br)Paul A. Souders/CORBIS; 81(tr)Bettmann/CORBIS, (br)Rudy Sulgan/Corbis; 82 (tl)P. Narayan/SuperStock, (tr)Bob Krist/CORBIS, (bl)Carl & Ann Purcell/CORBIS; 84-85 (b)Rubens Abboud/Alamy; 84 (t)Paul A. Souders/CORBIS, (tr)Rob Howard/Corbis, (cl)Alec Pytlowany/Masterfile; 85 Michael Klinec/Alamy; 88 MMH; 89 Dennis Cox/Alamy; 90 (tl)Bettmann/CORBIS, (tr)Danita Delimont/Alamy, (c)POPPERFOTO/Alamy; 91 (tl)Peter Turnley/CORBIS, (tr)Charles O'Rear/CORBIS, (c)Andrew Silk/Zuma/Corbis; 92-93 Fridmar Damm/zefa/Corbis; 92 (bcl)Adriane Van Zandenbergen/LPI, (bcr)SuperStock, (br)Charles O'Rear/CORBIS; 94-95 (tr)Adriane Van Zandenbergen/LPI; 94 (cl)Peter Titmuss/Alamy, (b)Charles O'Rear/CORBIS; 95 (t)Roger de la Harpe/Gallo Images/Getty Images, (bl)Hannelie Coetzee/Masterfile; 96 (tl)SuperStock, (tr)imagebroker/Alamy, (cl)Thomas Dressler/Superstock; 97 (tr)Arco Images/Alamy, (cr)Eric Nathan/Alamy; 98 (tl)Charles O'Rear/CORBIS, (bl)Steve Hamblin/Alamy, (c)Charles O'Rear/CORBIS, (br)Willie Sator/Alamy; 99 (t)Charles O'Rear/CORBIS, (b)Patrick Durand/CORBIS SYGMA (cr)Fridmar Damm/zefa/Corbis; 100-101 Digital Vision/PunchStock; 102-103 David Turnley/CORBIS; 102 (bl)Nigel J. Dennis; Gallo Images/CORBIS, (bcl)THE BRIDGEMAN ART LIBRARY, (bcr)Dave G. Houser/Corbis, (br)Associated Press; 103 Nigel J. Dennis; Gallo Images/CORBIS; 104 (tr)Jon Arnold Images/Alamy, (b)THE BRIDGEMAN ART LIBRARY; 105 (tl)Zen Icknow/CORBIS, (tr)Dave G. Houser/Corbis, (br)Eleanor Bentall/Corbis, 106 Associated Press; 107 (t)Peter Turnley/CORBIS, (cl)ADIL BRADLOW/AP Images, (bkgd)David Turnley/CORBIS; 108-109 Charles O'Rear/CORBIS; 108 (bl)David Sanger Photography/Alamy, (br)Digital Archive Japan/Alamy; 109 (cr)AP Images, (br)David Sanger Photography/Alamy; 110 (tl)Digital Archive Japan/Alamy, (bl)Reuters; 111 Charles O'Rear/CORBIS; 112-113 Andreas Stirnberg/The Image Bank/GettyImages; 112 (bl)AP Photo, (bcl)Greatstock Photographic Library/Alamy, (bcr)travelstock44/Alamy, (br)Louise Gubb/Corbis; 113 (cr)Kitt Cooper-Smith/Alamy, (br)AP Photo; 114 (t)dpa/Corbis, (b)Greatstock Photographic Library/Alamy; 115 (bl)travelstock44/Alamy, (br)Paul Springett/Alamy; 116 (tr)Bill Bachmann/Alamy, (b)Louise Gubb/Corbis; 117 (t)Yadid Levy/SuperStock, (cr)Andreas Stirnberg/The Image Bank/GettyImages; 119 Jose Fuste Raga/CORBIS; 120-121 Greatstock Photographic Library/Alamy; 120 (bl)Jose Fuste Raga/CORBIS, (bc)PCL/Alamy, (br)Reuters/CORBIS; 121 (br)Jose Fuste Raga/CORBIS; 122-123 (inset) (bkgd)Richard T. Nowitz/CORBIS; 122 (t)PCL Alamy, (b) travelstock44/Alamy; 123 (tr)Peter Titmuss/Alamy, (bl)Jon Hicks/Corbis; 124-125 imagebroker/Alamy; 124 (tr)Reuters/Alamy, (br)Jon Arnold/DanitaDelimont.com; 125 (t)Visual&Written SL/Alamy, (b)Greatstock Photographic Library/Alamy; 128 MMH; 129 Hideo Kurihara/Alamy; 130 (tl)Giraudon Art Resource, (tr)Travelshots.com/Alamy, (b)SuperStock; 131 (tl)SuperStock, (tr)Wojtek Buss/SuperStock, (b)Louvre, Paris, France/Giraudon/The Bridgeman Art Library; 132-133 John and Lisa Merrill/Corbis; 132 (bcl)Richard Broadwell/Alamy, (bcr) (br)Robert Harding Picture Library Ltd/Alamy; 133 Photodisc/PunchStock, 134 (bl)Peter Arnold, Inc./Alamy, (br)Richard Broadwell/Alamy; 135 (tl)CuboImages srl/Alamy, (tr)Stock Italia Alamy, (b)nagelestock.com/Alamy; 136-137 CORBIS; 136 (tr)Robert Harding Picture Library Ltd/Alamy, (cl)Juliet Coombe/Lonely Planet Images, (inset)Mark L Stephenson/CORBIS; 137 (tl)Paul Almasy/CORBIS, (tr)Claudio Beduschi/CuboImages/Robert Harding; 138 (tr)Photolocate/Alamy, (b)CuboImages sri/Alamy; 139 (t)Robert Harding Picture Library Ltd/Alamy, (b)John and Lisa Merrill/Corbis; 140 (bl)Sandro Vannini/CORBIS; 142-143 Free Agents Limited/CORBIS; 142 David Sanger Photography/Alamy; 143 THE BRIDGEMAN ART LIBRARY; 146 (tl)David Sanger Photography/Alamy, (cl)Art Resource, NY, (br)Alinari Archives/CORBIS; 147 (t)Art Kowalsky/Alamy, (bkgd)Free Agents Limited/CORBIS; 148-149 Vario images GmbH & Co.KG/Alamy; 148 (bl)LUCA ZENNARO/epa/Corbis, (br)STRINGER Italy/Reuters; 149 LUCA ZENNARO/epa/Corbis; 150 STRINGER Italy/Reuters; 151(tr)Ian M Butterfield/Alamy, (b)Vario Images GmbH & Co.KG/Alamy; 151 (tl)GIUSEPPE GIGLIA/epa/Corbis; 152-153 Julian Nieman/Alamy; 152 (bl)CuboImages srl/Alamy, (bc)ML Harris/Alamy, (br)CuboImages srl/Alamy; 153 (tr) (br)CuboImages srl/Alamy; 154-155 Massimo Listri/CORBIS; 154 (cl)ML Harris /